DISNEY CULTURE

QUICK TAKES: MOVIES AND POPULAR CULTURE

Quick Takes: Movies and Popular Culture is a series offering succinct overviews and high-quality writing on cutting-edge themes and issues in film studies. Authors offer both fresh perspectives on new areas of inquiry and original takes on established topics.

SERIES EDITORS:

Gwendolyn Audrey Foster is Willa Cather Professor of English, and she teaches film studies in the Department of English at the University of Nebraska, Lincoln.

Wheeler Winston Dixon is the James Ryan Endowed Professor of Film Studies and Professor of English at the University of Nebraska, Lincoln.

Ian Olney, *Zombie Cinema*
Valérie K. Orlando, *New African Cinema*
Steven Shaviro, *Digital Music Videos*
John Wills, *Disney Culture*

Disney
Culture

JOHN WILLS

RUTGERS UNIVERSITY PRESS

New Brunswick, Camden, and Newark, New Jersey, and London

Library of Congress Cataloging-in-Publication Data
Names: Wills, John, 1971– author.
Title: Disney culture / John Wills.
Description: New Brunswick, New Jersey : Rutgers University
Press, [2017] | Series: Quick takes: movies and popular culture |
Includes bibliographical references and index.
Identifiers: LCCN 2016032171| ISBN 9780813589138 (hardback) |
ISBN 9780813583327 (pbk.) | ISBN 9780813583334 (e-book (epub))
Subjects: LCSH: Walt Disney Company—Management. |
Corporate culture. | BISAC: PERFORMING ARTS / Film &
Video / History & Criticism. | SOCIAL SCIENCE / Popular
Culture. | SOCIAL SCIENCE / Media Studies.
Classification: LCC PN1999.W27 W55 2017 |
DDC 384/.80979494—dc23
LC record available at https://lccn.loc.gov/2016032171

A British Cataloging-in-Publication record for this book is
available from the British Library.

∞ The paper used in this publication meets the requirements of the
American National Standard for Information Sciences—
Permanence of Paper for Printed Library Materials,
ANSI Z 39.48–1992.

www.rutgersuniversitypress.org

Manufactured in the United States of America

CONTENTS

DISNEY CULTURE

INTRODUCTION

On December 21, 1937, Walt Disney's *Snow White and the Seven Dwarfs* premiered at the Carthay Circle Theater in Los Angeles, California. Disney's first feature-length animation had taken over three years to produce and, at $1,400,000, cost more than most movies of the day. Industry critics had nicknamed it "Disney's folly." At the gala event, Hollywood celebrities rubbed shoulders with Disney mascots: Shirley Temple, Charlie Chaplin, and Cary Grant stood alongside Dopey, Sleepy, and Sneezy. A couple of blocks from the theater, a movie-themed diorama called Dwarfland, complete with diamond mine and working water wheel, entertained crowds. Inside the auditorium, the first showing of *Snow White* began. Scenes of the evil queen speaking to her magical mirror and lovable dwarfs chanting "Heigh-ho" enthralled the audience. Walt Disney received a standing ovation. RKO-Pathe News reported on how the whole of "filmland thrills to Snow White" and declared the Hollywood opening "the most spectacular of them all." Attending the Radio City Music Hall premiere in New York City, Frank Nugent for the *New York Times* enthused over the "delightful fantasy," assuring readers that "Mr. Disney and his amazing technical crew have outdone themselves" ("Music Hall"). As the movie opened across the country, Snow White fever took hold. By May 1939, Disney's first feature-length film had amassed $6,740,000 in ticket sales, making it the most successful movie at that time in America. *Time* magazine deemed *Snow White* a magical, timeless piece of cinema, "as exciting as a Western, as funny as a haywire comedy, . . . to be shown in theaters and beloved by new generations long after the current crop of Hollywood stars, writers and directors are sleeping where no Prince's kiss can wake them" ("Mouse and Man").

The success of *Snow White* helped cement the Disney brand in American culture. Disney Studios had released its first sound cartoon film, *Steamboat Willie*, starring Mickey Mouse, in 1928. Within a decade, Walt Disney had gone from a little-known animator to a household name. Thanks to the characters Mickey Mouse and Donald Duck and the *Silly Symphonies* series, Disney emerged as a dominant force in entertainment in the 1930s. President Franklin D. Roosevelt watched Mickey Mouse cartoons in the White House, while abroad, Japanese Emperor Hirohito wore a Mickey Mouse watch (and owned a hobby horse named Snow White). The Disney label was synonymous with family fun, childhood, and the American Dream.

Indicative of the rise of popular animation, the youth of the 1930s became the "Mickey Mouse generation." Disney invaded not just the movie theater but store product lines, the American home, and even national consciousness.

In 1938, the journalist Douglas Churchill interviewed Walt Disney about his work on *Snow White*. Churchill was interested in "Disney's philosophy," the unique set of ideas that informed his studio's approach. Disney replied, "All we are trying to do is give the public good entertainment." However, the manufacture, content, and distribution of *Snow White* clearly said otherwise. The 1930s marked the ascendency not just of Disney animation but of Disney Culture.

Broadly speaking, "culture" is the sharing of symbols, beliefs, and ways of thinking. In 1993, the scholar Chris Rojek suggested that we might see Disney as a "culture," highlighting how Disney films and parks "support a specific moral order which is heavily moralistic and which presents 'The American Way'" (121). For Rojek, Disney promoted a "particular and historical form of white, capitalist society as the essential society of reason and good" (122). But how exactly does "Disney Culture" work? On a basic level, Disney Culture is the culture surrounding the Disney brand. It includes all Disney products, corporate and work practices, education, slogans, media, and advertising. Disney Culture incorporates such popular terms as the "Disney way" and the "Disney smile." It high-lights Disney's vision. It combines artistry, business, and family values. Disney Culture promotes a distinctive way of viewing the world. It provides immersion in childlike fantasy and simulation (Disney magic), facilitated by media, technology, and control (the Disney way) and mass consumption (Disney dollars). Disney Culture rests on the assimilation of other stories and ideas (the world according to Disney) that are reduced to impart a range of traditional and progressive values. It is these Disney val-ues, of a white, capitalist majority view, to which Rojek refers. Put simply, Disney Culture is our culture reshaped by Walt Disney: it is a Mickey Mouse take on the world.

Practically, we immerse ourselves in Disney Culture every time we engage with Disney media, from watching ABC television or Marvel movies to purchasing a *Frozen* figurine from the Disney Store or frequenting a Disney theme park. Ideologically, it is how we frame things in a Disney way, dream of living like a "Disney princess," or use Disney as our popular referent. Walt Disney first developed his "philosophy" at his studio on Hyperion Avenue in the late 1920s, where he introduced a distinc-tive work culture and story technique. Early Mickey Mouse cartoons reveal the evolution of a Disney way: a way of tackling the world based around clever animation, prankishness, and naïve sentimentality. With *Snow White* in the late 1930s, the Disney message grew significantly in both reach and sophistication. *Snow White* preached traditional gender roles and old-fashioned morality. Disney Culture has developed over time, sporting new priorities and shifting values. Today, Disney Culture is far more expansive and diffuse than ever. It can be seen in the myriad entertainment entities owned by the Walt Disney Company; by the global network of cruises, theme parks, TV channels, and toy stores; and by the generations of people raised on a diet of Disney. It can also be seen in the replication of "the Disney way" in corporations, schools, and family life around the world. The Disney Institute sells "Disney Culture" as a business model for corporations, while many theme parks and shopping malls resemble sanitized Disney realms. For Alan Bryman, this latter process represents the "Disneyization" of society, whereby Disney both influences and exemplifies new trends in consumer life. As one Disney worker contends, "The Sun never sets on Disney" (Carr).

Disney thus represents far more than simply "good entertainment." Disney exerts a powerful influence over our education, our values, and our lifestyle choices. As Alexandre Bohas contends, "For several generations, Disney has maintained a quasi-monopolistic position over Western youth culture." Disney Culture intrinsically shapes our world. While broadly considered "safe for kids," the Disney message is neither apolitical nor ahistorical. Over the years, the Walt Disney Company has been linked with anti-trade-union activity, McCarthyism, wartime propaganda, conservative family values, and suppressing critical filmmaking (for example, Michael Moore's *Fahrenheit 9/11*). It has equally been accused of promoting a liberal media bias and a progay agenda.

Given the historical influence of Disney Culture, it offers a valuable insight into understanding American culture across the twentieth and twenty-first centuries. Disney is tied to American iconography, childhood experience, popular cinema, suburban family values, social conservatism, and also change. The rise of Disney reflects the rise of both visual culture and consumer culture in the twentieth century. Disney Culture is tied to popular forms of patriotism and progressiveness. For some people, Disney is the essence of the American way. The Disney critic Stephen Fjellman labels Walt Disney World in Florida "the most ideologically important piece of land in the United States" (10). At around twenty million visitors a year, the entertainment complex is arguably the most visited place on earth. Both Disneyland and Disney World represent national pilgrimage sites, places of worship and devotion, with the cult of Disney verging on religion. Disney functions as a mecca for the middle class. To be American is to "do Disney."

This book serves as an introduction to the world of Disney. It uses the concept of Disney Culture to understand the rise of a true multimedia giant through the twentieth century and into the twenty-first century. Chapter 1 explores the technical creation of "Disney magic": the art, the animation, and the man. Chapter 2 considers the role of assimilation in Disney and explores Disney's relationship with both the United States and Europe. Chapter 3 then turns to practical matters: the making of Disney dollars. Chapter 4 looks at the core values embedded in Disney Culture, as well as some of the challenges and controversies involved.

• • •

Walt Disney's *Snow White and the Seven Dwarfs* presents an ideal opportunity to observe Disney Culture at work. As an early studio project and one that Walt Disney himself carefully oversaw, it reveals the development of ideas, practices, and vision that we now firmly associate with the company. The movie owes much to Walt's determination to perfect an alternate cartoon universe, a heavily caricatured realm to export to the real world. Dissecting the production of *Snow White* gives us a valuable first glimpse into Disney Culture. The movie contains all the core elements of that culture: the assimilation of a classic story using new ideas and new technology, the promotion of a movie using modern consumer marketing, and the

coupling of *Snow White* with notions of universal happiness, childhood naiveté, and cultural tradition. *Snow
White* also provided a valuable escape from the pressures
of the day.

First and foremost, *Snow White* resulted from a Disney way of manufacture that synthesized artistry with
control. Walt Disney first explained his ideas for *Snow
White* by personally acting out scenes of the movie before
his animators. His studio functioned as both an industrial factory and an artist's retreat: a realm of Taylorist
management and Fordist assembly-line production but
also intense artisan creativity. Walt developed his own
factory-like glossary of animation techniques (Scheuer,
"Cartoon Films"), insisted on the utmost loyalty and
dedication from his staff, and exercised total control. The
movie's most memorable song, "Heigh-Ho, Heigh-Ho, It's
Off to Work We Go," attested to the studio work ethic that
conjured it. This was clearly the Disney way. A drive for
perfecting Walt's unique and at times indulgent vision of
the classic fairy tale led to two million drawings and huge
financial outlays (for example, $100,000 expended on the
drawing of Snow White's two cartoon dresses). It also
entailed the harnessing of innovative methods and modern technology (or what I call Disney magic). Animators
matched musical scores to cartoon animal performance
and employed a multiplane camera to foster a striking

three-dimensional effect. The end product demonstrated unparalleled detail and immersion. The *Los Angeles Times* hailed *Snow White* a "masterpiece," pronouncing the movie "the greatest forward step in motion pictures since the advent of sound" ("Snow White Hailed").

A successful vision was coupled with successful distribution. The business acumen of Walt Disney could be seen in the shrewd marketing of his first animation feature. Coupled with the cinematic release, Disney encouraged a veritable merchandise bonanza. The company granted 147 movie tie-in licensees; 2,183 novelty items saturated the market; 16.5 million "Snow White" drinking glasses and 20 million books were sold (Pryor, "Snow White Sidelights").

On first seeing *Snow White*, Frank Nugent elevated Disney animators to the status of "modern magicians" ("One Touch"). Certainly for some people, *Snow White* appeared a work of pure wizardry, a cinematic world that blurred the boundaries of fantasy and reality. One housewife wrote Disney, "To settle a family argument please tell us whether or not three characters in 'Snow White' were real people or were drawn by your artists. I maintain that Snow White, the Prince, and the wicked Queen were all real actors, but my husband says I'm crazy" (Pryor, "Snow White Sidelights"). With *Snow White*, Disney provided an alluring fantasyland to escape both the daily grind of the Great Depression and the growing tensions on the eve of World War II. The movie proffered a potent "tonic for disillusion" (Nugent, "One Touch"), a filmic Prozac for the masses. As Nugent shrewdly observed, "Wars are being fought as the picture unreels; crimes are being committed; hatreds are being whetted; riots are being brewed. But the world fades away when Mr. Disney begins weaving his spell, and enchantment takes hold" ("One Touch").

Snow White was also the world according to Disney: a realm of fluffy creatures, domestic goddesses, and "whistle while you work." The film imparted conservative principles, teaching its audience the worth of traditional gender roles and absolute morality. It boasted decidedly Disney values of venerating childlike simplicity and sentimentality. The movie also entertained some intriguing ideas about nature and the environment, with Snow White uniquely able to converse with the local forest creatures that protect her from danger.

The film borrowed heavily from Old World folklore. Walt Disney feverishly purchased all kinds of European texts in the 1930s and set about converting them into cartoon fantasies. His team refashioned *Snow White* into a story centered on affable animals, singing dwarfs, and magical mirrors. As with many subsequent movies, the success of *Snow White* rested on a process of assimilation:

the Disneyfication of existing cultural products and their retelling and ultimate resale. *Snow White* was a European fairy tale reimagined through Disney Culture and exported to both US and international markets. As the journalist Mae Tinee commented at the time, a classic Grimm fairy tale had been "Walt Disney-ized." In turn, the Disneyized Snow White was herself assimilated by those audiences and, on occasion, even rebranded.

Snow White traveled the globe. Translated into ten languages, the movie played in forty-one countries. As with Mickey Mouse, Disney's *Snow White* pioneered cultural globalization. Not every country initially welcomed the US import. In Britain, for example, film censors feared an outbreak of child nightmares on exposure to the Wicked Witch and at first backed an age-sixteen rating. One newspaper explained how English children were "more easily upset by fairy stories than their 'tougher' American cousins" ("British Fear"). Nonetheless, the English adopted *Snow White* and assimilated Disney into their culture. In Salford, northern England, for example, Chief Constable Major C. V. Godfrey, representing the local city police force, obtained permission from Disney to incorporate the seven dwarfs in his road-safety campaign. Over the summer of 1939, Godfrey printed thirty-six thousand copies of his hand-drawn safety sheet for school kids, visiting four schools per day to promote a perfect "Snow White accident record" across the region. The safety sheet featured the seven dwarfs sharing nuggets of road-safety information ("Keeping the Sheet Snow-White").

Back in the United States, Disney Culture and American culture intertwined. The annual Tournament of Lights competition at Newport, California, featured a decidedly Disney theme when female contestants were asked to be the best Snow White. The appropriately named Miss Maurice Shipp won the naval-themed accolade and rode out on a spectacular "enchanted forest" barge during the water parade. Shipp also received a *Snow White* painting signed by Walt Disney. *Snow White* fever led to the seven dwarfs "receiving as much fan mail as the biggest stars in the film colony" of Hollywood ("Snow White Continues"). Political cartoonists realized that Disney Culture could be used to comment on real-world events. One newspaper doodle presented President Franklin D. Roosevelt as Prince Charming, economic recovery as Snow White waiting to be kissed, and the seven dwarfs as a range of economic integers (Pryor, "Snow White Sidelights"). In another satirical cartoon, Disney was used to comment on impending world war, with Snow White transformed into 'Jet Black' representing Nazi Germany and adjoining countries serving as her dwarfs (Pryor, "Snow White Sidelights"). Nugent for the *New York Times* meanwhile offered a more optimistic take on the impact of Disney Culture, claiming that "one touch of Disney makes the whole world kin" and that "Mr. Disney is our foremost ambassador of good-will" ("One Touch"). For Nugent, Disney seemed capable of making the world a better place.

1

MAKING DISNEY MAGIC

The Disney story (and with it Disney Culture) begins with Walt Disney's early forays into animation as a teenager in the late 1910s. Following a stint as a Red Cross driver in France, Disney took on a range of animation posts in the Midwest for Pesmen-Rubin Art Studio and Kansas City Film Ad Company, while also working on his own business projects, including Iwerks-Disney Commercial Artists (with fellow animator Ub Iwerks) and Laugh-O-Gram Studio comedy series. His early productions included *Tommy Tucker's Tooth* (1922) dentistry cartoon and short adaptations of the fairy tales Little Red Riding Hood and Cinderella. However, none of these ventures made significant profit, and in October 1923 at the age of twenty-one, a bankrupt Disney relocated to Hollywood, where he set up the Disney Brothers' Studio with his brother Roy on Hyperion Avenue. An intriguing mix of cartoon and live action, Disney's *Alice Comedies* provided the fledgling studio with some income, but distributor problems limited success. In 1926, the Hyperion studio refocused on the character of Oswald the Lucky Rabbit, producing a range of Oswald cartoons for Universal. However, in February 1928, Walt Disney lost the rights to Oswald during a fee renegotiation. Disney purportedly declared, "Never again will I work for somebody else" (Holliss and Sibley 14). Early productions featured at least some of the staples of classic Disney. Anthropomorphic lions sharpened their fake teeth, and Alice rode a Disneyland-style train in *Alice's Wonderland* (1923). Early Disney also featured a strong Charlie Chaplin–style comedy and a propensity for violence that was absent in later productions.

Part of Disney mythology is the story that Walt allegedly came up for the idea of Mickey Mouse on the return train journey from the Universal meeting in New York in which he lost the rights to Oswald. Working closely with Ub Iwerks, he promptly produced three short black-and-white Mickey Mouse cartoons. On November 21, 1928, Disney showed *Steamboat Willie*, a Buster Keaton–style romp, at Colony Theater, Los Angeles. *Variety* reported, "Giggles came so fast at the Colony that they were stumbling over each other," and predicted, "If the same combination of talent can turn out a series as good as *Steamboat Willie* they should find a wide market" (Landry). Mouse frenzy soon erupted. From Hollywood,

Philip Scheuer reported a sudden loss of work for slapstick comedians, with "animated cartoons replacing humans in Briefies" ("Mickey Mouse Routs"). Everyone wanted Mickey Mouse cartoons and memorabilia. By 1935, the Hyperion studio had grown to a staff of over three hundred. Disney began work on a number of feature-length animated movies, lavishing attention on cartoon versions of European classics *Snow White* and *Pinocchio*, as well as the Austrian Felix Salten's nature story *Bambi*. The rapid growth of Disney generated new problems. A five-week-long labor dispute in 1941 led to mass picketing at the new Burbank studio's entrance. Walt responded with Capone-style Mafiosi and intrusive surveillance of staff. Disney never forgave the strike organizers and later targeted them in anticommunist hearings.

During World War II, Disney produced a range of government propaganda movies. A consummate patriot, Walt rebranded his mascots as American heroes fighting the Nazis. Most famously, *Der Fuehrer's Face* (1943) parodied the German threat by relating the trials and tribulations of Donald Duck in "Nutzi Land," a fascist metropolis marked by manicured swastika shrubbery, razor-sharp bayonets, and authoritarian rule. Trapped in Nutzi Land, Donald finds himself forced to read *Mein Kampf* and practice his "Heil Hitlers" at gunpoint. The ruthless Nazi war machine takes its toll on Donald. Endless work at the local shell factory causes the duck to experience a mental breakdown. He then wakes up in his US flag pajamas, with the Statue of Liberty shining reassuringly through his window and Nutzi Land revealed as a nightmare. *Der Fuehrer's Face* roused anti-Nazi sentiment across the United States; it also revealed the Disneyfication of war. Disney propaganda reshaped world conflict into Chaplinesque cartoons awash with German stereotypes, swastika iconography, and incessant parody. With *Der Fuehrer's Face*'s catchy tune and lighthearted, even cathartic qualities, the film was more tongue-in-cheek than hard-hitting. While hardly on the front line, Disney Studios played a key cultural role in denouncing fascist aggression. Uncle Walt played a cartoon version of Uncle Sam. However, the combined cost of wartime propaganda and high-cost movies such as *Bambi* (1942) left the studio out of profit, with a debt of $4.3 million at the end of 1945.

In the postwar period, the Disney portfolio expanded to include live-action movies, nature documentaries (Disney's True-Life Adventures), regular television broadcasting, and theme parks, in the guise of Anaheim's Disneyland. Walt's enthusiasm for new projects proved remarkable. The 1950s represented a high point for Walt Disney and Disney Culture. Fans flocked to the newly opened Disneyland, while *The Mickey Mouse Club*, a variety show for kids, welcomed its first Mouseketeer performers. Through such actions, fans became not just distant spectators but active participants in all things Disney. The range of live-action hits included *Treasure Island* (1950), *20,000 Leagues under the Sea* (1954), and the TV series *Davy Crockett* (1954–55).

The immense success of Disney came down to a range of factors: shrewd marketing, technical excellence, musicality and comedy, and emotional impact. Disney connected with ideas surrounding childhood, the rise of television and cinema, the growth of consumer culture, and a national predilection for nostalgia and utopianism. Disney also provided escape, especially in periods of struggle. The early success of Mickey Mouse coincided with the Great Depression; now Disney prospered as entertaining respite from the Cold War.

Walt Disney himself emerged as champion of conservatism as well as McCarthyism. An FBI informant, Disney testified before the House Un-American Activities Committee on October 24, 1947, smearing a range of organizations and former employees as enemies of the state. As the business diversified and expanded, Walt spent less and less time on animation, with the demands of the Disneyland TV show taking its toll (he moaned, "Once you are in television, it's like operating a slaughter house. Nothing must go to waste. You have to figure ways to make glue out of the hoofs"; Schumach). In 1961, the

Disney company for the first time operated loan-free and in profit. On December 15, 1966, Walt Disney died of cancer. The Disney songwriter Richard Sherman called Walt a futurist and a great salesman; the science-fiction author and friend Ray Bradbury declared him "an American original," while President Lyndon B. Johnson remarked, "It is a sad day for America and the world" (Thomas 382).

The death of Walt Disney created a huge creative and directional vacuum. Walt's brother Roy O. Disney, Donn Tatum, and Card Walker initially ran the company but focused primarily on finishing Walt's projects, including Walt Disney World, Florida (opened in 1971). Infighting, lack of vision, and staff loss undermined the studio. Rather than push new animation, the corporation increasingly depended on live-action films for revenue. In the 1960s, Disney made just four animated movies out of around fifty releases: a trend that continued for the next two decades. New animations recycled old material, with *Fox and the Hound* (1981) replicating scenes from both *Bambi* and *Sword in the Stone* (1963). Alongside live-action hits such as the VW Beetle classic *The Love Bug* (1968), Disney produced a range of poor-quality B-movie productions, forgettable films such as *The Apple Dumpling Gang Rides Again* (1979). At the same time, the studio rejected offers to make both *Raiders of the Lost Ark* and *ET: The Extra Terrestrial*.

By the early 1980s, stagnation had set in. With the resignation of board director Roy E. Disney (Walt's nephew) and an investment of $500 million by the Bass Brothers, the future of the company seemed unsettled. Takeover bids loomed. In 1984, Michael Eisner took over as chief executive officer and marshaled a new corporate turn. Eisner revamped management structure, expanded product lines, and oversaw new Disney franchises and features. Profit jumped from $97 million net to $700 million net between 1984 and 1989. Eisner oversaw the "Disney Renaissance" of 1989 to 1999, a decade-long period of movie hits including *The Little Mermaid* (1989) and *The Lion King* (1994) that combined fresh characters with classic Disney animation.

Disney continued its corporate expansion into the twenty-first century. The Disney Channel found form with the teenage programs *Hannah Montana* and *High School Musical*, while new parks opened in Hong Kong and Shanghai, as well as the California Adventure next to the original Disneyland. In response to the rise of Pixar, "neo-Disney" dropped older styles of animation, introduced more complexity to its stories, and diversified topics, releasing both Western and science-fiction cartoons. For the scholar Chris Pallant, this change represented a more experimental Disney (125). In 2006, Disney purchased the cartoon giant Pixar. Pixar's John Lasseter promised to bring innovation and energy to the studios. In 2010, Disney produced its fiftieth animated feature, *Tangled*, which took in $591 million worldwide. In 2013, Disney's *Frozen* proved an even bigger success, netting over $1 billion. For the film journalist Scott Mendelson, the movie about two royal sisters amounted to "Disney's triumphant reaffirmation of its cultural legacy."

The Disney story is a story of an evolving corporation, culture, and brand. A variety of impulses lie behind Disney Culture. Walt Disney's personal vision, coupled with the immense popularity of Mickey Mouse, determined the early studio's direction. A unique blending of art, music, and technology contributed to the success. The Disney universe also relies on subtle systems of control to offer an alluring and immersive escape.

A "MICKEY MOUSE" STORY

In twentieth-century Disney, two figures dominated the company: Walt Disney and Mickey Mouse. Walt Disney famously related, "It all started with a mouse" (Disney Studios, *What Is Disneyland*). Disney business, vision, and culture all derived from the drawing of one cartoon figure. According to Walt, Mickey Mouse was not just the technical beginning of a successful Disney brand but at the heart of it all. Mickey Mouse cartoons proved important to Disney Culture as they set the tone of the studio. Playful, childlike, animal focused, and family oriented, Mickey Mouse features proved decidedly mainstream entertainment, and Mickey became the ideal consumer product to export.

The rise of Mickey Mouse corresponded with the dawn of Disney Culture. Walt was inspired by his pet mouse, Mortimer, to imagine a new mascot to replace Oswald the Rabbit. Ub Iwerks drew Mickey as a simple character with broad appeal. Imagining him to be similar to the contemporary Felix the Cat, Iwerks described Mickey as "the standardized thing" (Brockway, *Myth* 130). Two silent movies, *Plane Crazy* (based on the Charles Lindbergh flight) and *The Gallopin' Gaucho* (inspired by a Douglas Fairbanks movie) followed, but the true breakthrough came with *Steamboat Willie* (1928), thanks in part to its remarkable soundtrack. Early Mickey Mouse cartoons proved slapstick-heavy, highly visual escapades. In *Steamboat Willie*, Mickey played animals as instruments and had few qualms about cruel and violent behavior. The scholar Stephen Jay Gould highlights how "the original Mickey was a rambunctious, even slightly sadistic fellow" (30).

Success changed the rodent. High demand led to a production line of Mickey Mouse cartoons and merchandise. Mickey quickly became more than a studio mascot: an American institution, a national hero, and a savior in the Great Depression. Mickey also became a product: a toy to take home, a wristwatch to wear. As the family fan base grew around the mouse, Disney felt under pressure to deliver a consistently wholesome role model. Born a trickster, Mickey quickly matured into a safe, family-friendly character. The more sensible rodent could be seen directing music in *The Band Concert* (1935), while Donald Duck assumed the role of trickster. Responsibility over Mickey (or, in Disney's words, the golden rule "not to mess with the mouse") translated into creative doldrums. Frustrated, Walt disclosed in 1934, "He's such an institution that we're limited in what we can do with him" (Brockway, *Myth* 131). The number of original Mickey features dropped. Mickey also began to look visibly different. Playing safe with the mouse led to a softening of Mickey's features, as evident in the big-eyed, loquacious Mickey in *The Pointer* (1939). He became more juvenile and less challenging. In both behavioral and aesthetic terms, Mickey reverted to childhood, went back to the womb. For Gould, the result was a "blander and inoffensive" mouse (30).

By the 1950s, Mickey Mouse had become more important to Disney as a corporate logo than as a movie character. With reference to the sociologist William H. Whyte's research into white-collar men of the time, "He became an 'organization man'" (Brockway, *Myth* 133). The journalist Edward Lewine went further, seeing Mickey as "a corporate prisoner, representing suppressed individuality in the name of image and profits." The revised, inoffensive appearance of Mickey reflected the direction that Disney as a whole was heading toward: mainstream products designed with maximum profit in mind. Mickey symbolized the new look of Disney Culture: his softer, simpler lines highlighting a company playing it safe. Mickey embodied the corporate image of Disney Studios.

In 1981, the artist Andy Warhol produced a series of ten screen prints titled "Myths" that included a portrait of Mickey Mouse alongside portrayals of Uncle Sam and Superman. Mickey Mouse stood tall as an icon of America. Like Warhol, Walt Disney had combined art, advertising, and commerce to frame popular culture. Mickey served as precursor to the logos of today: Apple, Microsoft, and Nike. The author John Updike declared Mickey Mouse "the most persistent and pervasive figment of American popular culture in this century" and a better symbol than even Uncle Sam for the nation. Certainly, alongside the Coca-Cola can and the golden arches of McDonald's, Mickey Mouse proved an eminent symbol of American culture in the twentieth century.

However, by the close of the century, most Disney fans wore Mickey ears, but few watched Mickey cartoons. An almighty symbol, Mickey curiously lacked a decisive role. In 1978, John Culhane for the *Saturday Review* wrote, "He would surely now be eager to blast off into the farthest reaches of outer space. Then woe be unto Darth Vader if he should venture so far out of his class as to kidnap Minnie Mouse!" Commentators pondered whether Disney could ever resurrect its archetypal cartoon character. Mickey Mouse in many ways seemed tethered to the Walt Disney years and appeared a relic of the past. The Disney biographer Bob Thomas saw in Mickey Mouse the "alter-ego" of Walt and a character irrevocably tied to the studio master (150). As Walt himself admitted, "He's a pretty nice fellow who never does anybody any harm, who gets into scrapes through no fault of his own, but always managed to come up grinning. . . . There's a lot of Mouse in me" (Updike). For the scholar Robert Brockway, Mickey proved as "complex as Disney was himself and as profound in his symbolic and mythic implications as any mythic or fairy tale character" ("Masks" 26). Certainly Mickey played a pivotal role in Disney's early success, as the journalist Marshall Fishwick concluded: "Mickey was Disney's Model T—simple, sturdy, and functional." However, one hundred years on, the Model T seemed decidedly outdated.

WALT DISNEY, HERITAGE, AND SELF-MYTHOLOGY

Walt Disney's personal interests—from his fondness for animals, circuses, and toy trains to his loyalty to conservative politics and small-town America—all shaped the fabric of the studio. His take on business, art, and animation determined the culture of the organization and, in turn, the values exported outside the studio and around the world. Disney invested a great deal into his projects, with the making of Disneyland being akin to "a crusade" (Thomas 254).

The popular image of Walt Disney is of a fatherly figure sitting at his desk enthusing about his latest project. Walt is cast as the great artist, the father of animation, and the inspiration behind literally hundreds of Disney cartoons. Fans imagine Disney handcrafting early pictures and sprinkling magical Disney dust on them. According to popular Disney mythology, Walt brought immense happiness to the world. The biographer Marc Eliot contends that a viewer can see much of Walt in his early movies, with Mickey Mouse operating as his superego and Donald Duck as his id (181–82). As one journalist remarked, "Disney pictures have a technique and a philosophy, but they would be headless horsemen, without the fervor of Walt Disney's spirit" (Ducas). Equally, California's Disneyland owes much to Walt's personal imagination. The park serves as a time capsule of 1950s Americana and a cryogenic freezing of Disney's fictions. Visitors enter a plastic and concrete realization of one man's fantasy, a world where a severed Lincoln head talks and giant rodents greet you. Like Lincoln, Walt Disney has become an American folk hero. Through his anticommunist stance, his wartime propaganda, his work ethic, his family values, and his strong sense of tradition, Walt provided a father-like, protective role to people living in uncertain times during the mid-twentieth century. Disney served as the nation's family man, welcome in every home, comforting to every child, and protector of all things good about the country. Hedda Hopper for the *Los Angeles Times* simply called him the "All-Year Santa Claus." Known affectionately as Uncle Walt, Disney promoted simple happiness as his philosophy. He provided an appealingly sentimental, nostalgic, and good-natured take on the world.

What lies behind the popular image of Walt Disney is less certain. A reclusive, private person, he is hard to know and a figure of controversy. Certainly he was far from the only influence on studio or park creations. He was neither the father of animation nor the inventor. Notable examples of animation that predate Disney include *The Enchanted Drawing* (1900) and *Humorous Phases of Funny Faces* (1906) by J. Stuart Blackton and *Fantasmagorie* (1908) by Émile Cohl. First seen in *Feline Follies* (1919),

Felix the Cat inspired the creation of Julius in Disney's Alice Comedies and Mickey Mouse himself. Nor was Disney the first to introduce sound or color to cartoons. He was very much part of a worldwide animation movement and competed alongside the likes of the Australian cartoonist Pat Sullivan. He never operated in a vacuum. Neither did Disney hand-draw his movies. Walt was in fact only a moderately good artist and gave up sketching in the late 1920s. While he oversaw myriad productions and collected twenty-six Oscars, he rarely put pen to paper. For Thomas, "Disney possessed a remarkable skill for drawing the best from those who worked with him" (xiv). As Sean Griffin contends, "Walt Disney so successfully performed authorship of his studio's output during his lifetime that many customers thought Walt drew all the cartoons himself" (141). Disney productions were typically a team effort, with an animation team nicknamed the "Nine Old Men" responsible for crafting most early movies. Revealingly, Disney likened himself to a "little bee . . . fathering pollen" in the studio, generating the image of one happy hive at Hyperion. Rosalind Shaffer reporting for the *Chicago Daily Tribune* in 1936 told how "a visit to Walt Disney's plant is almost like a visit to Santa Claus' toy factory at the north pole, with the sole exception that the ice is left out." In reality, the quality and tactics of Walt's "fathering" varied dramatically, from inspirational leadership to

dictatorial control. In June 1935, he sent memos to thir-
teen animators personally lambasting their work (Barrier
112), yet he clearly adored his team.

Behind the cameras, Disney was a worrier, a perfec-
tionist, a workaholic, and a chain-smoker. He suffered
a number of nervous breakdowns. Diane Disney Miller
captured both sides of Walt when describing her father
as "generous, kind, overworked, and sometimes given to
outbursts of temper." Rather than the mythic figure portrayed in television and the movies, Disney could also
be quite normal. On interviewing Walt, Dorothy Ducas
reported, "He is fond of badminton and lowbrow music;
he seldom reads a book and never paints or draws for
art's sake," and he ultimately appeared a "typical busi-
nessman." Opinion remains split on how progressive he
was. Some critics have denounced Disney as a racist and
an anti-Semite, citing his involvement with the Motion
Picture Alliance for the Preservation of American Ideals
in the 1940s, a pro-American, anticommunist group of
filmmakers, as well as his use of a Jewish "peddler" stereo-
type as the Big Bad Wolf in *Three Little Pigs* (1933). Others
highlight Disney's employment of a range of Jewish artists and his role as a donator to Jewish charities, including the Hebrew Orphan Asylum of the City of New York
(made up of thankful, "enthusiastic Mickey Mouse fans";
Pierce). Disney's contribution of happiness to the world

has also been questioned. Rather than offering dreams of utopia, for Chris Rojek, Walt Disney gifted a "bland, homespun philosophy" (122) to the masses. Arguably, Disney characters and consumers alike have been caught in Walt's fantasy for years.

Ultimately, the legend of Walt Disney is a product of Disney Culture itself. Much of the positive imagery of Walt came from the Walt Disney Company, an organization already functioning as a well-oiled mythmaking machine. Alongside Cinderella and Alice in Wonderland, the studio forged a fairy-tale version of its own lead character. For a corporation keen to celebrate its history, mythologizing the creator came naturally. A heavily nostalgic institution transformed its own leader into a god. The Walt Disney Company made Walt Disney myth. Whether or not Disney himself wanted to be a "story character," through his regular TV appearances Walt became larger than life. He became a lasting folk hero.

Protecting the reputation of Walt Disney remains a company priority in the twenty-first century. In response to growing questions about Walt's character, the studio released the biopic *Saving Mr. Banks* (2013). Tackling the making of *Mary Poppins* (1964), the movie depicted a charming (but fabricated) courtship between Walt Disney and the author P. L. Travers. *Saving Mr. Banks* was in essence "Saving Mr. Disney." While the movie

revealed the extent to which Disney Studios still idealized its founder, not everyone in the audience agreed
with the rose-tinted assessment. At the National Board
of Review Awards, the Hollywood star Meryl Streep
spoke angrily of the "real, not reel, Disney," while Walt's
relation Abigail Disney declared, "*Saving Mr. Banks* was a
brazen attempt by the company to make a saint out of the
man" (Feinberg).

ART, MUSIC, AND TECHNOLOGY: CREATING GOOD STORIES

Art, music, and technology proved crucial to the rise of
Disney Culture.

The studio sports a history of innovation based around
the employment of new technology and animation techniques, while the incorporation of distinctive musical
sketches proves crucial to its enduring appeal. The company has harnessed art, music, and technology to craft
highly commercial, family-friendly movies. Rather than
offer niche, high-culture pieces, its projects remain based
around middle-class culture and mass interest. Disney is
one of the most successful mainstream creative studios
in existence.

Early Disney cartoons attest to a studio focused
more on mainstream draw than artistic accomplishment.

Alongside Mickey Mouse, most 1920s Disney projects displayed a simple design quality. Their originality and aesthetic qualities came from perfectly choreographed performance, as in the rhythmic motion of skeletal bones in *The Skeleton Dance* (1929). Disney also liked to animate the unanimated, granting cars personalities in the Oswald the Lucky Rabbit cartoon *Rival Romeos* (1928). The studio's focus on movement worked so well with early cinema that in spite of the lack of sophisticated artistry, Disney himself was heralded as a hero. In 1934, the *Nation* declared Mickey Mouse the "supreme artistic achievement of the moving picture" (Schwarz), while for the cartoonist David Low, Walt Disney amounted to "the most significant graphic artist since Leonardo da Vinci." Disney's shift to feature movies corresponded with a new desire of Walt to forge a lasting, influential impact on cinema. *Snow White*, *Pinocchio*, *Bambi*, and *Fantasia* all took several years to create, with an anxious Walt overseeing each picture with meticulous attention to detail. Together, the four films reflected the creative maturation of the studio and a breakthrough in animated cinema. They cemented a sense of a distinctively Disney artistry. Disney entered a new "serious realm" of entertainment ("Disney Invades"). In 1938, both Yale and Harvard bestowed the honor of Master of Arts on Walt Disney. In 1939, the Metropolitan Museum of Art in New York City displayed original watercolor artwork from *Snow White*. The curator Harry B. Wehle imparted his enthusiasm for Disney: "I think he is a great historical figure in the development of American art" and "probably the greatest popular artist of this generation" ("Disney Joins").

A fusion of classical music and rodent high jinks, *Fantasia* (1940) more than anything highlighted Walt's willingness to experiment with artistic forms and to traverse traditional boundaries. Brockway views the movie as evidence of the "artistic idealism" of Walt Disney: "Money is important indirectly, experimentation comes first" (*Myth* 132). The product of Walt's relationship with the composer Leopold Stokowski, the movie showcased Disney's highest artistic aspirations. Stokowski hoped that *Fantasia* "may be a quickening influence" on the attainment of a better life for all (Allan 94). The film promoted a distinctly "Disneyfied" form of high culture, with Mickey conducting a range of musical sketches, and targeted those who had never entered a concert hall. *Fantasia* presented Mickey as an inspiration to all.

The limited financial success, as well as time-intensive nature, of Disney's first animated movies nonetheless pushed the studio toward an altogether more commercial path. The 1940s saw a lasting shift in Disney from artistic experimentation to commercialism. Cheaper, simpler, less artistic movies such as *Dumbo* (1941) became the norm. Profit won over perfection in the postwar period. Disney himself lamented the shift to cheaper techniques, berating the Xerox drawing for movies such as *101 Dalmatians* (1961). As Benjamin Schwarz maintains, "The safe, the bland, and—to a large extent—the mindless comforting" took over. Once fans of Disney, the cultural elite not only deserted Mickey Mouse but came to loathe him. However, the mainstream audience continued to welcome Disney into their homes.

The musicality of Disney represents another key part of Disney Culture. From *Snow White*'s "Whistle While You Work" through to *Frozen*'s "Let It Go," the cartoon studio has worked its way into the popular consciousness of a nation through a series of eminently catchy tunes. From the beginning, Walt realized the value of music as both a timing instrument and a storytelling device. The physical humor of the early studio's black-and-white cartoons worked precisely because of the intricate timing of animation to music. The success of *Steamboat Willie* owed much to its "musical animals" and the synchronicity of sound and animation. Scenes included a goat eating a newspaper with notes playing as they fell to the floor and Mickey using a duck as bagpipes and the teeth of a cow as a xylophone. The frame-by-frame matching of sound to visuals (nicknamed "Mickey Mousing") advanced the notion of movies having their own rhythm and flow. In commercial terms, Disney's music compilation from *Snow White*, titled "Victor's Songs," served as one of the earliest movie soundtracks and helped popularize the format. In the 1960s, the Sherman Brothers began writing soundtracks for Disney motion pictures. Their work included songs for *Mary Poppins*, *The Jungle Book*, *Chitty Chitty Bang Bang*, and *Bedknobs and Broomsticks*. From the 1990s onward, the Disney power ballad, in the guise of songs such as "Beauty and the Beast," performed by Celine Dion and Peabo Bryson, and "Can You Feel the Love Tonight," composed by Elton John for *The Lion King*, became a staple of children's parties and karaoke bars. Much of the cultural memory of Disney resides in music and song. As *Forbes* magazine concludes, "a huge portion of the legendary 'Disney magic' is due to their songs above all else" (Mendelson).

Technical innovation also marks Disney Culture. John Updike saw Walt Disney as "one of those great Americans, like Edison and Henry Ford, who invented themselves in terms of a new technology." He mastered innovative methods of film animation and introduced them to the American public. The Disney brand became synonymous with groundbreaking cartoons. Following *Steamboat Willie*, Walt forged an exclusive deal with Technicolor on his

Silly Symphonies series (1929–39). For both *Snow White* and *Pinocchio* (1940), he employed a multiplane camera to create three-dimensional effects. For *Fantasia*, the studio developed its own sound system (Fantasound) to mimic an orchestra. Disney also perfected the mixing of live action and cartoon in movies such as *Mary Poppins* and *Who Killed Roger Rabbit?* (1988). Meanwhile, live-action movies drew on the latest special effects, as in early computer animation in the cyber-cycles of *Tron* (1982).

The technical innovation included theme parks. Disneyland resembled an interactive film set. The park took its cues directly from the entertainment industry, with the Hollywood set designer Harper Goff responsible for the look of Frontierland's Western saloons and Adventureland's Jungle Cruise. Similar to the scientific utopianism of world's fairs, the park extolled the virtues of a technological future. Early plans for Disneyland highlighted how the park would offer "a new experience in entertainment," with guests transported by moving sidewalks, accompanied by interactive animatronic figures (Disneyland brochure, 1953). Disneyland celebrated the fantasy of a technological America. However, the mood never got too serious. As the scholar David Allen contends, any serious message aside, "shows were actually a demonstration and celebration of the power of 'Imagineering'" (33). Technology remained confined to entertainment.

PIXIE DUST, ESCAPE, AND SIMULATION

Much of the appeal of Disney Culture rests in its facilitation of escape. Disney magically whisks people away from their daily toils and transports them to new worlds and places. It meets a mass desire for flight. As revelers at Coney Island amusements fled the urban pressures of New York City in the early 1900s, the company has offered reprieve from the Great Depression, World War II, the Cold War, and the War on Terror. Like a new religion for the consumer masses, Disney has offered hope in times of difficulty across the twentieth and twenty-first centuries. As the Soviet filmmaker and film theorist Sergei Eisenstein proposed in 1941, "Disney is a marvelous lullaby for the suffering and unfortunate, the oppressed and deprived" (88). Fjellman describes Disney as an "antidote to everyday life" (11), while upon visiting Las Vegas and Disneyland in the 1950s, the journalist Julian Halevy decided, "both these institutions exist for the relief of tension and boredom, as tranquilizers for social anxiety, . . . fantasy experiences in which not-so-secret longings are pseudo-satisfied." Disney amounts to a mass comfort blanket.

The "Disney escape" relies heavily on processes of transformation and simulation. Walt Disney once described his art as sprinkling pixie dust on things ("Disney magic" might equally describe the same alchemic practice). This "dust" or "magic" has specific properties: it transforms the ordinary, the tired, the non-Disney into the child friendly, the fun, the quintessentially Disney. Disney gives things a fresh lease on life and makes them interesting. The pixie dust also reveals Disney Culture as a process of transformation, even renewal, with varying degrees of impact. Sometimes, the technique amounts to little more than rebranding or repackaging existing sources—Disney's Marvel or *Star Wars* franchises for example. On other occasions, the transformation can be fundamental: the end product little resembling its origin, as in the case of Disney's *Pocahontas* (1995) and its reinterpretation of colonial encounters.

The exact form of "escape" varies in content but remains Disney by its look, symbols, and referents. Typically the studio produces a wholesale "simulation" for us to engage with: a magical domain to enter or a cartoon fantasy to adore. Walt Disney explained that "the first duty of the cartoon is not to picture or duplicate real action or things as they actually happen—but to give a caricature of life and action—to picture on the screen things that have run through the imagination of the audience—to bring to life dream-fantasies and imaginative fancies that we have all thought of during our lives" (Thomas 120). The corporation thus aims for a mass fantasy, a total simulation neither quantifiably real nor unreal—a liminal space that we can all comfortably jump into, especially in its parks.

While the audience directly experiences escape, "reality" is not always as it seems. Disney is a master of illusion. As with historic amusement parks that lured visitors into crooked houses and mirrored rooms, Disney prospers in its fakery. Like Busch Gardens in Tampa and Knott's Berry Farm in Buena Park, Disney theme parks offer adventure without risk and simulations of danger. Disney offers a fake and hyperreal world: a realm of three-dimensional realizations of two-dimensional cartoons, a land of mimicry and facsimile. Fairy-tale castles transport visitors to magical lands where "every girl can be a princess." Source material is identified and Disneyfied for the masses. It is changed, redesigned, and re-presented. Everything is simulacrum (or imitation): history, nature, nostalgia, money, America, and even smiles. For Jean Baudrillard, Disneyland represents "a perfect model of the entangled orders of simulation" (*Simulations* 23), a realm based purely on popular representation.

Part of the appeal of the escape is precisely this façade of exploration and danger. Audiences act out good-versus-evil scenarios, chuckle when villains falter, and take part in heroic fantasy narratives. They have a role. Disney provides a safe and coherent illusion, with clear borders and strict rules. There is a fundamental predictability and reassurance to it. The fake also appeals precisely due to its fakery. Both architect and audience are keenly aware of the "illusion" at play. Jungle Cruise guides engage in self-conscious adult humor, designed to highlight the facsimile at work, explaining to guests, "we're on a low budget," and pointing out the harmlessness of natives wielding spears. Disney is decidedly postmodern and self-referential, providing a dislocated realm of imagination. As David Allen sees it, Disney operates a "reality game": "The Disney park does not simulate the 'real'; rather, it celebrates the art of the simulation, the ability to construct fantasy worlds as if they are 'real'" (34). Visitors admire the plastic crocodiles as recognizably fakes. They admire the creativity and the artistry behind heavily stylized versions of life but consciously differentiate the original and the mimic. Most tourists are under no illusions: they know Disney Main Street is not a real Main Street, nor Frontierland the real Wild West.

The fake Disney version can nonetheless sometimes seem preferable to the real thing. On a trip to the United States in the 1970s, the Italian philosopher Umberto Eco appreciated Disneyland's New Orleans far more than its Louisiana counterpart. For some people, the sanitized Disney "fake" provides a better version of the original. Like Las Vegas, Disneyland presents popular symbols and images of the United States. Arguably, Disney sells a simulated America to the masses: a hyperreal and improved version of itself. For Baudrillard, Disney, America, and the image/fake are all tied together very closely. "Disneyland is presented as imaginary in order to make us believe that the rest is real, when in fact all of Los Angeles and the America surrounding it are no longer real, but of the order of the hyperreal and simulation" (*America* 25). Thus, for Baudrillard, Disney is not the exception but the rule: rather than an island of Disneyfied America, Disney *is* in fact America exemplified. Baudrillard's comments are situated in a dialogue of Old World versus New World bias, with America unfairly cast as a realm without history, culture, or depth.

Putting aside the parks' fakery, they nonetheless function as fully fledged experiments in Disney Culture: domes of social imagination (and control). As if magnetically attracted to a Disney core, Paul Rodaway observes how park visitors "enter into a kind of ecstatic trance" (260). Both literally and figuratively, they buy into a simulation built around animatronics and cartoon imagery. Exiting their cars, they leave behind the old world, reality, the "outside," and willingly travel by electric bus to a new world, the fictive, the fantasy. A berm of artificial foliage divides the two zones. Upon arrival, guests debark and pass through iron gates into a new world. Colors change, money shifts form, even the popular lexicon transmutes into Disney phrases. They enter Disney Culture in its purest form: an immersive realm that vanquishes seriousness, real-world problems, and danger and instead thrives on fun, childhood, and facsimile. The park is where Disney simulates "culture," where a Disneyfied take on US society is at its best. Over the years, the company has created a distinctively Disney simulation (or Dis-world) with its own codes, values, and belief systems. Disneyland residents are impeccably polite, while the trains arrive and depart on time, and everyone smiles. The perfection of Disney Culture inside the parks lies in its internal coherence, its look, its surface, and its storytelling capacity. The perfection also depends on rules. For those who are caught inside the Dis-world (be they employees, customers, or visitors), all perform according to a set of codes.

As experiments in Disney Culture, the parks offer significant rewards. They are realms of enjoyment, safe play, happiness, and rapture. They are (relatively) crime-free, drug-free, and harmonious landscapes. They inspire creativity and wonder. Dying children make it their last wish to visit Disneyland or Disney World. For the majority of people, a trip to Disney is a trip of a lifetime. With Mickey Mouse pandering to the whims of young children and the photographic needs of adults, the Disney experience hardly resembles a Kafkaesque nightmare. As the art historian Cher Knight explains, "Visitors to Disney World are not duped by its simulations but are savvy consumers of these" (20). Guests assimilate Disney: they actively determine their own fulfilling recreational experience.

By contrast, critics portray these landscapes as confused, discombobulated, and empty experiences, superficial worlds of two-dimensional buildings and a multiplicity of plastic and anodyne. Disney service culture grants the illusion of being welcome, but without the warmth or authenticity. The Marxist theorist Fredric Jameson sees Disney as the epitome of postmodern "depthlessness." The strictness of Dis-world also creates its own set of challenges. Maintaining the perfect illusion entails huge effort. Hundreds of employees work through the night at Disney theme parks. The "dark side of Disney" is a realm of night gardening, gum cleaning, fence painting, and feral cats (around two hundred at California's Disneyland alone). Workers clean food remnants off Main Street and saliva off rides. The manager David Caranci describes how "it's a city that never sleeps," a clear allusion to Las Vegas (Martin). Employees find themselves not allowed to "refer to things outside the Disney realm" (Cast-member). Only things Disney exist in Disney. In that way, Dis-world presents a form of "total institution." The sociologist Erving Goffman defined the total institution as an all-encompassing, closely administered sphere of life, exemplified by prisons and

hospitals. The Disney experience taken to its natural conclusion amounts to a Mickey Mouse monoculture that is
far from inclusive, that breeds a form of mass conformity
and control.

For critics, the properties of the Disney escape also
pose a danger to our individual imagination and to our
culture "outside." Through parks, films, and games, Disney asks the audience to leave their real world behind for
uniform childlike fantasies and simulations. The company
provides us with all we need: a supply of "imagination"
for us to consume. Rather than having to forge our own
visions, Disney provides Americans with an alluring collective vision to which to escape. Spoon-fed from birth
on a diet of such programing (thanks to channels Disney Junior and Disney XD), children no longer learn to
imagine for themselves. For Jennifer Cypher and Eric
Higgs, Disney is caught up in a "colonization of imagination" (109). Grappling with an excess of hyperreality and
sensory overload, we are threatened by such hegemony
with a loss of "us." Starting as a culture of distraction and
escape, Disney becomes the mainstream reality. Everyone
wants to be a Disney princess or a Disney *Star Wars* character. With the fantasy so immersive, Disneyphiles spend
increasing time in a *Matrix*-like existence of cartoon
characters and Hannah Montanas. Disney, in a sense,
takes over. In this regard, the corporation is a symbol of a

broader cultural transition toward virtual, digital, and fantasy-based hobbies and lifestyles that are dominant in the twenty-first century. Disney Culture is to a large degree part of a greater shift toward digital fantasies.

THE DISNEY WAY OF CONTROL

So far, I have touched on the "Disney way" in the guise of the leadership of Walt, the mascot of Mickey, and the contribution of art, music, technology, and simulation to the business. There are other approaches that help elucidate Disney Culture. Alan Bryman views the "Disney way" as a rational and calculated process involving four specific techniques: theming, hybrid consumption, merchandizing, and performative labor. For Bryman, Disneyization represents a "systemscape" of such principles. Popularized by Disney, the systemscape can be found "diffusing throughout the economy, culture, and society" (vii). Bryman also deems control and surveillance as crucial to the corporation's success. The landscape theorist Alexander Wilson has highlighted how the Disney way is to "whimsify" life, transforming everything into entertainment capital (182). All these factors might be seen to contribute to Disney Culture. The Disney way further entails the Disneyfying of behavior: the making of Disney people.

For the company's staff, Disney signifies more than a job: it is a brand, a philosophy, and a work culture. Since 1955, Disney University has educated citizens in the Disney way, trained people to be effective "cast members" (terminology for the company's employees). At the "University," cast members learn about the common beliefs, aims, and community surrounding Mousedom. There, the company defines Disney Culture as "the values, myths, heroes, and symbols that have a significant meaning to the employees": "Ours is a culture that is so strong it has withstood the test of time and is recognized all over the world" (Wasko 92). Orientation meetings for cast members introduce them to the importance of heritage (labeled "traditions"), the ethos of "We create happiness," and a range of service guidelines. In 1965, Disney introduced the "Four Keys": "safety," "courtesy," "show" ("I stay in character and perform my role in the show"), and "capacity" (or running efficiently). Disney later remodeled the "keys" around the Seven Dwarfs, adding such instruction as "Don't be Grumpy. . . . Always display appropriate body language at all times." Disney puts great store by these guiding principles, "the foundation for everything Disney does" ("Disney's Four Keys"). However, with the exception of "show," the Disney keys remain remarkably generic and similar to those of other major US corporations. At Coca-Cola, the aims of "passion," "boundless opportunities," and the "chance to make a difference in the world" seem little different ("Unique Culture"), as do the beverage company's seven core values: leadership, passion, integrity, collaboration, diversity, quality, and accountability ("Mission, Vision and Values"). Starbucks's emphasis on the cultural experience of coffee drinking strikes a similar chord.

Walt Disney corporate trainers explain, "We don't put people in Disney, we put Disney in people" (Lukas 187). Corporate culture employs techniques to strip away the "self" of employees and remake them as "Disney cast members." Markers of individual identity (tattoos, jewelry, long hair) are hidden or removed. Reminiscent of Goffman's concept of the "mortification of self" that happens at total institutions such as psychiatric hospitals, cast members lose themselves and gain a new identity. Employees learn the Disney look, Disney language (or what might be called Dis-course), and Disney behavior (or way). The "Disney Look Book" imparts specific rules governing aesthetics, including forbidding tattoos that show and allowing hair only in a "classic, easy-to-maintain style" (Disney College Program). Cast members learn a new "Dis-guise." Employees face instant dismissal if caught publicly removing their costumes. Disney language is rich in slogans and keywords, such as "Magic" and "Imagineering." It is also remarkably positivist. For example, Bruce Jones, programing director at the Disney Institute, explains how he uses "'the 3 o'clock parade' question," a request for simple directions, "to help Cast Members understand that their answer can either end the conversation, or it can *begin a quest for a richer discovery*." Given that many employees act out movie characters, Disney work culture is performative and theatrical (Bryman terms this "performative labor"; 103). Deviation from script is unwelcome. For some employees, the pressures to abide can prove burdensome. As one former "Snow White" complained, "There's lots of rules. It's why people get so frustrated working there, you're always worried about getting in trouble" (Willett). Some scholars have interpreted Disney work culture as primarily a philosophy of control.

In order to optimize profit and efficiency, as well as to keep the illusion intact, control is built into the visitor experience. To a degree, people are the biggest problem for the Disney universe. As at national parks, where the wilderness is threatened by its own popularity and ecological vulnerability, at Disneyland the perfect experience is jeopardized by the presence of too many mouse-eared fans wandering the kingdom. The "Happiest Place on Earth" requires active preservation and governance to prevent its degeneration. Visitors are expected to play roles just as much as cast members do. Those napping on benches are politely told to get up (happiness is not equated to a short nap), disruptive influences told to leave, and intrusive technologies banned (for example, selfie sticks in June 2015). Disney works hard to keep human traffic (or, in corporate parlance, "guest flow") at an optimum level, with one-way sidewalks introduced at peak times.

The parks also employ illusion to maintain control: many illusions provide ways to manage customers. On the classic Jungle Cruise ride, Boat Skippers talk to queuing guests to distract them from the wait, managing expectations and frustrations and ultimately keeping people in a holding pattern. "Illusion" justifies private ambulances and private security.

Control also factors into Disney's decision to embrace new surveillance technology. In 2005, the company introduced geometric fingerprinting readers at its Orlando park. Although short of full fingerprinting, park-based readers gather information on visitors that could be used by the National Security Agency or law enforcement. Such control arguably casts customers as potential criminals, rather than guests. Other technical innovations highlight the increasing synchronicity of Disney Culture and modern surveillance culture. In February 2011, Disney funded $1 billion for its "Magic Band" wrist device. Dubbed "a virtual key to the Magic Kingdom,"

the electronic band promised a more interactive and easier experience at park resorts (Carr). Thanks to the band
relaying important information, cast members could welcome visitors to restaurants by name (the "Be Our Guest"
program) and offer a far more personal experience. The
Magic Bands promised, as if by "magic," to organize a trip
itinerary from arrival in Orlando onward, opening hotel
doors and rendering the wallet archaic. Disney's Magic
Bands pointed toward new levels of knowledge and control: better command of parkscape, the flow of people,
and the flow of money. The Magic Band functions as a
credit card, whereby Disney tracks you but you lose track
of your money.

The "Disney way" thus can seem both liberating (in
terms of escape) and also prescriptive and at times con-
trolling. For Disney workers and visitors alike, total
freedom is the key illusion. Chris Rojek argues that the
Disney "leisure experience operates to organize subjects
rather than enabling them to exercise free choice and
self-determination" (122). For Umberto Eco, Disneyland
remains "a place of total passivity. Its visitors must agree
to behave like robots" (48). Henry Giroux even alludes to
Disney as a postwar "Auschwitz" (55). However, scholars
forget that historically a multitude of other, non-Disney
parks have exercised class control or applied principles
of betterment, Central Park being a case in point. Disney

visitors are neither automatons nor victims of a Machiavellian mouse with a master plan. Whatever the rules, visitors manufacture their own experiences. A small minority deviate from the Disney way, sneaking food in or even hiring disabled people to circumvent queues. Many guests make Disney their own, subverting Disney language (from "Disney drivers" to "Mickey Mouse operations") or wearing Disney as a retro fashion statement. And the vast majority simply enjoy the Disney experience.

2

THE WORLD ACCORDING TO DISNEY

Originally designed for Pepsi at the 1964 New York World's Fair, Disneyland's It's a Small World provides a water-based fifteen-minute journey across the globe. Three hundred audio-animatronic children chant the ride's title song in their "native" language, a Sherman Brothers message of peace crafted in response to the Cuban Missile Crisis. The song is arguably the most played music in history. It's a Small World underlines the common values of humankind and a shared destiny on this planet. It also situates Disney at the core of those values, the force that binds the world together and makes it small. Disney Culture is a powerful force connecting the United States and the world. It communicates across territorial, religious, political, and cultural divides. The studio often does this by a process of *assimilation*, whereby it takes a multitude of stories and adapts (or Disneyfies) them for an international audience. Disney remains a major culture producer for the globe.

DISNEY AND EUROPE

European influences can be seen across myriad Disney cartoons and live-action productions. Applauded as "a modern Hans Christian Andersen" in one 1937 interview, Walt Disney replied, "Oh no, Andersen was the originator. We've only taken the memories of our childhood and recreated them for the screen" (Schallert). His earliest cartoons such as the *Alice Comedies* proved heavily indebted to the European market. Disney's *Skeleton Dance* (1929) appeared inspired by the stop-motion film *Le squelette joyeux* (1897) by the French Lumière brothers. Most studio hits, especially in the Walt Disney era, proved conversions of popular European stories. *Snow White* came from the Brothers Grimm (Germany 1812), *Alice in Wonderland* from Lewis Carroll (England 1865), *Peter Pan* from J. M. Barrie (Scotland 1902), *Pinocchio* from Carlo Collodi (Italy 1883), *Cinderella* from Charles Perrault (France 1697), and *The Hunchback of Notre Dame* from Victor Hugo (France 1831). In the live-action realm, *20,000 Leagues under the Sea* originated from Jules Verne (France 1870), *Robinson Crusoe* from Daniel Defoe (England 1719), *Swiss Family Robinson* from Johann David

Wyss (Germany 1812), and *Treasure Island* from Robert Louis Stevenson (Scotland 1883).

An expert on the studio's European links, Robin Allan contends, "The Disney product is indebted to an older cultural heritage; Disney absorbed and recreated that heritage for a new mass audience" (1). Walt Disneyfied his European source material: simplifying narrative, adding new characters and creatures, introducing comedy and music, and highlighting the sentimentality. He transformed tired and overfamiliar stories into spectacular and exciting movies. Disney fed the Hyperion and Burbank studios with European folklore, and out came cartoon blockbusters. For Allan, this process amounted to a "new art form" (xv).

European example also factored into the design, development, and expansion of Disney theme parks. Early plans for Disneyland (first labeled "Mickey Mouse Park") drew on European precedents of recreation first refined at Hampton Court and Versailles. While the homegrown Coney Island, with its tawdry look and criminal vices, depressed Walt Disney, European parks inspired him to create Disneyland. On visiting Tivoli Gardens in Copenhagen, he enthused, "Now this is what an amusement place should be!" (Thomas 251). European folklore similarly determined the park's content. Studio promoters described a trip to Disneyland as "like Alice stepping through the looking glass" (brochure 1953). With rides based around King Arthur, Snow White, Peter Pan, and Pinocchio, Disneyland's Fantasyland in particular provided an exploration of fantasy Europe.

Through such projects, the studio not only reengineered European folklore but produced a fictional, highly Disneyfied, and highly Americanized Europe that proved popular on both sides of the Atlantic. In the case of the movie *Pinocchio*, animators added a chatty insect with Chaplinesque behaviors, Jiminy Cricket, to guide the Italian puppet-boy. A wish-granting Blue Fairy resembling Jean Harlow referenced US glamor girls of the period. London's *Observer* called the studio's 1953 adaptation of *Peter Pan* simply "Pan-American" (Allan 222). The pirate Long John Silver (played by Robert Newton) in Disney's *Treasure Island* (1950) spoke with a distinctive American-English patter that quickly became the standard movie "pirate voice."

With *Mary Poppins* (1964), the studio showcased a fantastical London awash with colors, clouds, and visual spectacle. *Variety* adored the "dream-world rendition" (Williams). With its Georgian townhouses and red pillar letterboxes, the movie offered a veritable treasure trove of London architecture. The British capital oozed with romance and history. It also suffered serious smog and seemed decidedly class ridden. Highlighting Disney's

political agenda, the movie offered incisive class commentary, exposing the viewer to the upper-class world
of ruthless business via the financier George Banks
(singing, "It's great to be an Englishman in 1910") and
the lower-class world of begging, dancing, and pigeon
feeding via the chimney sweep Bert (played by Dick Van
Dyke). Disney's movie consistently trumpeted the under-
class. A jab at British hunting culture, one scene showed
Banks's rebellious children aiding a distinctly Irish-voiced
fox escape killing. The author P. L. Travers expressed huge
disappointment with the movie. The Disneyfied London
reemerged in a surfeit of movies, including *Bedknobs and
Broomsticks* (1971).

The Disneyization of so many European stories reflected Walt Disney's own interest in European travel
along with his avid collection of storybooks. For Umberto
Eco, the studio's popular reproduction of European folk
stories revealed something much bigger and more worrying: a country desperate to establish itself on a cultural stage. According to Eco, Americans wanted their
own towering castles and Old World inheritance, and
awash with cultural anxiety, "the ideology of this America wants to establish reassurance through imitation"
(23). Rather than an "American original" as claimed by
Bob Thomas, Walt Disney seemed a pretend hero, and
his stories amounted to simplistic rehashes of European

history. However, Eco missed how far Disney transformed European story into American story and how the stories changed. The success of Disney highlighted the rise of American culture, not its duplicity. As Yosemite and Yellowstone competed with European cathedrals for world attention, Disney World's Cinderella Castle rivaled the ancient citadels across the pond. The same vignette of cultural nationalism that led the nature writer John Muir to proselytize the wonders of Yosemite equally applied to Walt Disney and Disneyland.

The response of Europe to Disney's creations proved initially hopeful. In the 1930s, Europeans welcomed Mickey Mouse as if one of their own. Mickey proved especially popular in Paris. The French newspaper *Le Figaro* adored the rodent. In 1935, the League of Nations awarded Walt Disney a medal. The early success of the studio in Europe owed much to Disney selling Europe to itself: the retelling of homegrown folklore aiding translation and popularity. Residents happily consumed Disney Culture. Mickey Mouse had become the new cultural ambassador for the United States. Alva Johnston, writing for *Woman's Home Companion*, proclaimed, "Charlie Chaplin and Mickey Mouse are the only universal characters that have ever existed," and "Mickey Mouse is not a foreigner in any part of the world." In a 1937 piece, the *New York Times* exalted Mickey as both "an internationalist" and an all-conquering "emperor of the world" (Russell). With the backdrop of approaching war, the *Times* presented Disney's rodent as a commanding leader, a cultural hero ready to scupper any nefarious plans: "The air armadas of Europe, the plunging submarines, the skittering destroyers and dignified battleships cannot compete with the creatures which Mickey can call forth to battle if he chooses. He can scuttle a pirate with the aid of a sawfish and turn tortoises into tanks." Seven years later, the Allies used "Mickey Mouse" as the password for the D-Day invasion of Normandy.

The growth of the Walt Disney Company in the postwar period nonetheless spawned fears of a different kind of invasion: of American takeover. Disney's expansion into Europe proved particularly contentious in the case of Disneyland Paris in the 1990s. CEO Michael Eisner initially declared France the "most enthusiastic of all countries toward Disney, its merchandise, its culture," highlighting how "Mickey Mouse is a star in France" ("Disneyland Gang"). Disney's Robert Fitzpatrick related, "My biggest fear is that we will be too successful" (Greenhouse). The hubris proved misplaced. On arrival in France, Eisner was met with eggs, ketchup, and "Mickey Go Home" placards. With illusions to the 1986 nuclear accident in Ukraine, project opponents nicknamed Disneyland Paris a "cultural Chernobyl" (Kehr). Once welcomed by the French,

Mickey Mouse had become a symbol of uncultured capitalism. Despite attempts to "Frenchify" the theme park, early attendance figures proved disappointing, with debts almost leading to closure in March 1994. As Fitzpatrick admitted, "Europe isn't North America" (Greenhouse).

Disneyland Paris revealed that despite hopes of "a small world," regional differences still remained. As Allan relates, "The overlay of American virtues of self-sufficiency, wish fulfillment—'when you wish upon a star'—and the attainment of a materialist happiness, sits uneasily upon a much older European moral tradition" (70). Europeans gradually came to fear the Disneyfication of home and the rewriting of folk stories. European reactions to Disney also reflected attitudes to American businesses more broadly. Just like Coca-Cola, McDonald's, Starbucks, and Microsoft, the Walt Disney Company was a US giant that threatened local businesses and native culture. Disneyfication seemed much the same as Cocacolanization or McDonaldization: the selling of the American Dream in a can, burger box, or caricature made little practical difference to European consumers. The golden arches, Coca-Cola script, and mouse ears attested to the same process of American goods taking over. The Burbank studio offended because it exported the New World to the Old World. Fear of Disneyfication jelled with greater fears of American capitalism.

Americanization and Disneyfication appeared synonymous and indistinguishable.

Testament to the might of Mickey Mouse, Michael Eisner once claimed that the Walt Disney Company helped
break down the Berlin Wall by its promotion of Western
ideology through entertainment. By contrast, for Giroux,
the studio instead threatened the creation of a "national
entertainment state" (46), led by an invasion force of
Mickey Mouse Clubs. A force for liberation or contain-
ment, Disney remains part of a broader cultural exchange.
Mickey Mouse is caught in a process of cultural conversation, assimilation, and counterassimilation. While the
Burbank studio has assimilated and transformed world
stories, so too have people around the world appropri-
ated both Mickey Mouse and the Disney brand for their
own uses, as in the case of the English constable's use of
Snow White's seven dwarfs in his road-safety campaign
(see chapter 1). Like McDonald's, Disney has embraced
cultural sensitivity and now adapts its products for local
markets, introducing wine at Disneyland Paris, feng shui
at Hong Kong Disneyland, and Mickey Mouse kimonos
at Tokyo Disney Resort. While some people may long
for the return of European stories to Europe, Disney has
ultimately used European folklore as a route toward truly
universal storytelling. Entering the twenty-first century,
the Disney story increasingly seems not so much about

America or Europe but about crafting a cohesive Disney *world*. Tied to neither Old World nor New World ideas, the corporation increasingly focuses on its own legacy and mission. This marks Disney as something beyond geographic borders. As the Disneyland ambassador (and former Miss Disneyland) Connie Swanson-Lane remarked, "I find that happiness is more or less international" (Mouse Clubhouse).

DISNEY AND AMERICA

A perimeter line marks the border between Disneyland, Anaheim, and the hustle and bustle of Los Angeles. Local residents travel from their gated communities to a world of limitless possibilities. Inside the park, they engage with all kinds of folktales, but most of all, they interact with one man's story. Disneyland is Walt Disney's story of America. With his Anaheim project, Walt re-created "America" as a Disneyfied theme-park experience, a DisAmerica. He set out his premise: "Disneyland will be based upon and dedicated to the ideals, the dreams, and the hard facts that created America" (Pryor, "Land of Fantasia"). Disneyland represented a shrine to the nation, a Mickey Mouse totem. As Walt confided, "I believe in emphasizing the story of what made America great and what will keep it great" (Giroux 35). For Rojek, Disneyland "is a story of the moral and economic superiority of the American way of life and it presents history as intrinsically progressive" (126).

Adamant that "this is not an amusement park" (Thomas 283), Walt Disney presented Disneyland as something altogether new and exceptional. In reality, the park connected with a long history of American entertainment. Influenced by a sizable knowledge of the US amusement industry and world's fairs, Walt conceptualized the park as a unison of existing types of attractions: "Disneyland will be something of a fair, an exhibition, a playground, a community center, a museum of living facts, and a showplace of beauty and magic" (Mosley 221). Despite his personal antipathy toward Coney Island, Walt's own park mimicked traditional fairgrounds. When Disneyland opened, it featured a range of arcades, penny machines, and carousel horses (the horses from Coney itself). A planned Lilliputian land resembled Coney Island's Lilliputian village of the 1900s.

Disneyland also functioned as a celebration of America of time gone by. It provided an interactive realm steeped in nostalgia, history, and romance. As a child, Walt Disney lived on a small farm in Marceline, Kansas. In a letter to the town crafted in 1938, Walt related his fond memories of childhood and his enthusiasm for home: "Everything connected with Marceline was a thrill to us. . . . I'm glad

I'm a small town boy and I'm glad Marceline was my town" (Allan 2). This love for Marceline filtered into Walt's plans for the park, in particular its central thoroughfare. Walt's granddaughter Disney Diane Miller explained, "Main Street in Disneyland is his dreamlike recreation of Marceline Main Street as he remembers it." Disneyland also peddled in nostalgia for a lost frontier. The themed land of Frontierland celebrated the old Wild West captured in film, a fictional kingdom of stagecoaches, river rapids, cowboys, and Indians.

The Walt Disney Company turned history into interactive entertainment that helped Americans feel good about themselves. Audio-animatronic figures reanimated history for audiences; former presidents of the United States spoke to the crowds. The studio breathed life into lost, dead, and departed historical objects. Disney tapped nostalgia for historic America and reminded visitors of "the good old ways." Perpetually producing positive images of where the nation had come from, the park thus operated as a timely propaganda machine. As Rojek sees it, Disneyland was "calculated to give a reassuring impression of history" (128) and only had room for positive histories. Disneyfied history thus meant "good history," with difficult topics such as slavery kept outside the berms.

Mike Wallace contends, "It is possible that Walt Disney has taught people more history, in a more memorable way, than they ever learned in school" (Fjellman 59). As a popular purveyor of the past, the Burbank studio has educated the masses in the story of the "buckskin Barbie" Pocahontas, the frontiersman Davy Crockett, and the American revolutionary Johnny Tremain. On television, at the movies, and in the parks, Disneyfied history has promoted a fun and triumphant understanding of the nation. Only occasionally has this proved controversial.

In November 1993, the company proposed an American-history-themed park in Haymarket, Virginia, "celebrating the nation's richness of diversity, spirit, and innovation" (Walt Disney Company). Disney's Bob Weis, who headed the development, labeled it "an ideal complement" to a history-rich area, located near the First Battle of Bull Run and just thirty-five miles southwest of the White House (Walt Disney Company). The park promised an intimate and realistic experience of key events of America's past. A Civil War–era village served as hub, leading out to a Native America world (navigated by a Lewis and Clark rapids ride), Presidents Square, Civil War Fort, Monitor versus Merrimack fight, Ellis Island, "Enterprise" town (complete with a roller coaster named the Industrial Revolution), a "Victory Field" of World War II airplanes, and finally a Coney-style fair. "Disney's America" promised a more nuanced, serious, and education-based Disney experience: "a venue for people of all ages, especially the young, to debate and discuss the future of our nation and to learn more about its past by living it" (Walt Disney Company).

The response proved unexpectedly hostile. Haymarket residents feared a "new Orlando" on their doorstep, highlighting the sprawl of housing, hotels, and pollution associated with the project. Citizens feared a historic region being "obscured and overrun by neon and franchises" (Kotz and Abramson). Concern centered on the park's content: specifically the notion of a *Disney history* park. The company's plan to create its own history project threatened the real American history on display. The documentary maker Ken Burns railed, "the area doesn't need any more history superimposed on it, especially of the intoxicatingly distilled kind Disney is proposing." The Virginia resident Graham Dozier rallied, "the REAL history is what draws people, not some silly plastic version of our past," confiding, "I have nightmares of Mickey and Donald wearing the blue and grey" ("Historians vs. Disney"). Supported by over two hundred academics and historians, including the Civil War experts Shelby Foote and James M. McPherson, Protect Historic America (PHA) launched an effective campaign against the Walt Disney Company. Members criticized the company's educational content, its financial motivations, its "sachariny sentimentality," and its inability to tackle serious issues ("Historians vs. Disney"). The novelist William Styron wrote to the *New York Times*, "I have doubts whether the technical wizardry that so entrances children and grown-ups at other Disney parks can do anything but mock a theme as momentous as slavery" (Perez-Pena). Robert Spore cried, "I don't want to see any more generations fed the cleaned up Disney version of history" ("Historians vs. Disney"). Protesters shrewdly pitted "History" versus "Disney." They argued that ultimately the corporation could not be trusted with the nation's past and that history would be lost to Distory.

The reaction shocked the Walt Disney Company. Eisner, who was hoping for the park as one of his legacies, was stunned by the negativity. In a defiant mood, the CEO charged, "If the people think we will back off, they are mistaken," and "The First Amendment gives you the right to be plastic" (Powers). Arguably, much of Disney's America had already been accepted in other media and formats, with many other popular versions of history out there. However, "Distory Park" offended because of its unusual combination of geography, local competition, and intention of "doing serious history." In September 1994, the studio dropped the project. Looking back, Eisner lamented how "the Walt Disney Company had been effectively portrayed as an enemy of American history and a plunderer of sacred ground" (337).

DISNEY AND THE 1950S

Opening Disneyland in July 1955, Walt Disney's claim in brochures, "You will find yourself in the land of yesterday, tomorrow, and fantasy. . . . Nothing of the present exists," underscored the sense of temporal distortion and escape offered by Anaheim's theme park. Disneyland offered a liminal space: a realm of time travel and shifting dreamscapes. Disney exceptionalism (the idea of the studio being quantifiably unique) underscored the idea of the park as separated and isolated from the real world. However, the park very much related to the contemporary period. Disney Culture mimicked American culture. The park's design incorporated new technological fascinations, corporate visions, and political ideas. The studio pandered to suburbanites and baby boomers. A popular zeitgeist shaped the parkscape. Disneyland provided a "1950s take" on American past, present, and future.

First and foremost, Disneyland was a Cold War park. The park resounded with Cold War values, celebrated the space race, and exhibited a range of American technologies and businesses. The park showcased American consumption and recreation in a similar vein to the American National Exhibition that ran in Moscow in 1959. On a state trip to the United States, Soviet Premier Nikita Khrushchev related great interest in Disneyland.

When he was denied access on security grounds, an angry Khrushchev challenged, "Why not? What is it, do you have rocket-launching pads there?" ("Premier Annoyed"). The Disney way—consumerist, capitalist, and individualist—stood as a populist antithesis to the Marxist/Soviet way. An architectural and highly symbolic statement of the American Dream, Disneyland exuded a highly exportable form of cultural nationalism. The park provided a bulwark of US cultural capital against Cold War communist aggression.

Disneyland also offered temporary refuge from the biggest fear of the Cold War: Armageddon. Prior to the 1950s, parks typically offered fleeting reprieve from the ardors of city life and urban pollution. The notion of escape took on a new totality and drama with the nuclear age. Fear of annihilation affected all kinds of building projects, inspiring covered shopping malls and home-built bomb shelters. Timothy Mennel argues that "utopian sites were shaped as much by Cold War concerns as by capitalist dreams" (116). Enclosed, controlled spaces provided symbolic protection from atomic attack. Disneyland offered a psychological bomb shelter for the masses: a duck-and-cover experiment with Mickey Mouse in the place of Bert the Turtle. Its berms divided fantasy America from apocalyptic America. Disney Culture fundamentally offered a culture of Cold War reassurance.

Disneyland also connected with new dominant trends of the period. An appendage to the rise of white middle-class suburbia, Disneyland offered a place where Americans fundamentally prospered. It provided a new consumer playground alongside Route 66 drive-ins and bustling department stores. The sociologist C. Wright Mills's research into white-collar work and "the salesman ethic and convention to pretend interest" equally applied to cast members on Main Street acting from scripts (82). Disneyland operated as a figment of white middle-class performance and consciousness.

The success of Disney projects in the 1950s reflected the synchronicity of Walt's ideas with the priorities of the decade. A committed anticommunist and conservative, Walt echoed many of the values prevalent in the period. With a mutual emphasis on conformity, control, consumption, idealism, conservatism, and naiveté, Disney Culture and American culture matched. One complemented the other. The 1950s represented the heyday of Disney Culture.

FUTURE AND DIS-TOPIA?

Postwar Disney Culture also proved successful because it captured a growing romance with utopian living, white cities, and new technology. Disney mapped out not just

America of the past but America of the future. Tomorrowland and later EPCOT transported visitors to a paradise just around the corner. A technological idealist, Walt
Disney committed WED Enterprises to create four exhibits for the 1964 New York world's fair, one each for Pepsi,
Ford, General Electric, and the state of Illinois. Walt
referred to WED as his "backyard laboratory": "I can do
things with WED without asking anyone, even my wife"
(Stroud). He deployed a range of studio technologies
(including audio-animatronics) to formulate the exhibits.
Along with Pepsi's It's a Small World, Disney created an
automotive-based future for Ford and a mechanical Abra-
ham Lincoln guide for the state of Illinois. For General
Electric, Disney constructed the Carousel (or Theater)
of Progress, a rotating six-stage story assembled out of a
decrepit dinosaur-themed exhibit. The Carousel showed
how electricity made life easier across the decades.
Throughout the ride, a Sherman Brothers song repeated,
"There's a Great Big Beautiful Tomorrow." The Carousel
epitomized the technological utopianism of Disney.

Disney linked new technologies to a new world. Caught
up in excitement over nuclear energy (what one CBS
radio broadcast labeled the "sunny side of the atom"),
like many corporations, Disney indulged in the unfolding atomic gold rush. Walt firmly declared on television
that "the atom is our future" (Walt Disney Studios, "Our

Friend the Atom"). Disneyland featured "atomic subma-rines" and the Monsanto-sponsored House of Tomor-row, a futuristic living space complete with an "Atoms for Living Kitchen." Distributed widely at schools, Dis-ney's educational film and book *Our Friend the Atom* tied nuclear developments to the ushering in of a brave new world. The program's guide, Dr. Heinz Haber, presented the discovery of the atom as akin to a fisherman finding a genie in a bottle. Haber situated nuclear power as part of a grand narrative of history, connecting the atom with scientists such as Aristotle and the recent advent of space exploration. The fully Disneyfied atom seemed "almost like a fairytale," a gift of "magic power" capable of saving the world (Walt Disney Studios, "Our Friend the Atom").

Such positivity reflected a broader aspect at work within the studio: the selling of an American future and a timely updating of the American Dream. The Walt Disney Company broadcast an American Dream for the twentieth century built around family, technology, con-sumerism, and convenience. Disney's articulation of the American Dream proved eminently persuasive in its car-toon packaging and Technicolor glow. "When You Wish upon a Star" served as a Disneyfied American anthem. The Burbank studio offered hope to the masses and a model of the future that was very different from Cold War scares or science fiction that depicted termination. The hope engine of America, Disney fulfilled child and adult dreams alike.

The success of Disney Culture in the twentieth century owed much to its alignment with the optimistic side of American mass culture. The company symbolized a fundamentally good, traditional, and enlightened America. For Brockway, Walt Disney was "attuned to the soul of Middle America" (*Myth* 132). He instructed citizens on values, goals, and aspirations in his weekly television programs. He was someone Americans could relate to. Disney served as the nation's twentieth-century storyteller and guide, a replacement for the likes of Benjamin Franklin and Mark Twain. His cartoon avatar, Mickey Mouse, came out "smiling through Depression, Wars, A-Bombs, and H-Bombs" (Jamison).

The Walt Disney Company was also something that Americans could rely on. The studio served as a US institution, a cultural cornerstone, and a comfort blanket for the nation. With generations of families taking their first trip to Disneyland and watching their first Disney movie together, Disney represented a collective cultural experience and a rite of passage. Benjamin Schwarz for the *Atlantic* recounted, "for better or for worse, Walt Disney (1901–1966) implanted his creations more profoundly and pervasively in the national psyche than has any other figure in the history of American popular culture."

At times, Disney Culture and American culture seemed almost the same. As the sociologist Robert Pettit argued, "Disney does such a wonderful job of representing American culture, they're almost synonymous with America" (Hetter). In 1971, at the peak of countercultural protest, the *Los Angeles Times* covered Grad Nite at Disney, whereby 110,000 students visited the park to celebrate college completion. Watched over by "our society's superparent figure, Walt Disney," the kids had a clean, drug-free, alcohol-free, family-friendly night, the kind of "party that would please a Southern Baptist convention" (Cartnal). Americans flocked to Walt Disney's sanitized and idealized version of their country. Schwarz concluded, "To be a mainstream American in the American century was to inhabit Walt Disney's world." There seemed nothing more American than Walt Disney.

CRITICISM: DISNEY AND THE RUINATION OF AMERICAN CULTURE

While for the vast majority, Disney Culture resembles American Culture at its best, for a small but vocal minority, the intersection between Disney and America proves less welcome. Indeed, homegrown concern over the studio dates back to the 1950s. In *The Holy Barbarians* (1959), Lawrence Lipton coined the term "Disneyfication" when writing "about the neon chrome artyfake Disneyfication of America" (144). For his contemporary Julian Halevy, Disney Culture threatened the ruination of American popular culture. "Life is bright-colored, clean, cute, titivating, safe, mediocre, inoffensive to the lowest common denominator, and somehow poignantly inhuman," he wrote of Disney. Traveling aboard the Jungle Cruise, Halevy came to the worrying and irrational conclusion that "one feels our whole mass culture heading up the dark river to the source—that heart of darkness where Mr. Disney traffics in pastel-trinketed evil for gold and ivory."

By the 1970s, the corporation increasingly seemed out of touch with national trends and growing diversity. Theme parks resembled landscapes of the white middle class, gated communities keeping out crime, class conflict, the disenfranchised, and the disempowered. Disney arguably resembled an apartheid world. It misrepresented the real America. Rather than adding to the nation, the Burbank studio seemed to be taking away. As Janet Harbord argued, "Disney is a form of memory-wiping, an amnesia in the face of a conflicted and violent twentieth century, and a refusal of other experiences of the present" (48). For Fjellman, the company offered "one version of the United States and its view of the world" (21). In December 2013, Walt's grandniece Abigail Disney related her disappointment with the brand: "What my family's business has done is to dumb down and middle-ify and oversimplify (ok, ok DISNEYFY) so much, and while that has rightly and admirably brought a lot of pleasure—joy even—to a lot of people who needed it given that life can be hard and pleasure hard to come by, it has also encouraged that most grim and American tendency to gloss over the untidy complexities of life, sometimes at great cost to the lived experiences of many others" (Feinberg). Arguably, Disney Culture had damaged American culture on a fundamental level.

3

DISNEY DOLLARS

In 1987, Harry Brice, a company employee who worked on Main Street, attended a local Disneyana Convention awash with mementos and collectibles. Watching person after person hand over their dollars, Brice had a eureka moment in the world of branding: why not pay for Disney with Disney? Rather than rely on Uncle Sam's money, Burbank fans could use their own Mickey-endorsed currency as tender. "Disney dollars" could also serve as a tradable souvenir and memento. On May 5, the first Disney dollars became currency at Disneyland, Anaheim.

Featuring Scrooge McDuck as treasurer and Tinkerbell as border motif, the Disney dollars transformed currency into entertainment. Reminiscent of Monopoly money, the cartoonish folding stuff presented capitalism as just a game and encouraged visitors to spend likewise. However, fully microprinted and sporting individual serial numbers, Disney dollars functioned as real currency.

Mickey Mouse and Goofy had replaced Washington and Lincoln as the new denomination of Mickey Mouse country. Disney dollars trumped real dollars. The act of printing its own currency placed Disneyland in the realms of nation-state. Unlike Monopoly money, park dollars had "foreign exchange" value and represented a sound investment. Original 1987 Mickey Mouse dollars attained tenfold, even hundredfold, exchange-rate increases against the US dollar. Disney dollars made money.

The introduction of Disney dollars exemplified the corporate nature of modern Disney. The Walt Disney Company serves as a model of successful entertainment capitalism. During Walt's oversight of the company, the studio rarely ran at a profit. Following his death, boardroom strategies and bank balances took over. As CEO Michael Eisner admitted in an internal memo in 1981, "To make money is our only objective" (Wasko 28). In the past forty years, the studio has grown to become the premier US entertainment provider. The tiny rodent represents a corporate goliath. Corporate Disney Culture prioritizes expanding portfolios, the assimilation (or Disneyfying) of competition, the maximizing of merchandising opportunities, and the theming of product lines. The studio also bears striking similarities with other major US companies such as McDonald's and remains a powerful symbol of American capitalism.

DISNEYFYING

Disney's aggressive corporate expansion beginning in the 1980s rested on tapping both new and established commercial fields. The corporate turn entailed extensive portfolio acquisition. The studio annexed conventional media brands, with Eisner backing the purchase of Miramax (1993) and ABC (1995). It increased its share of adult cinema with the development of Touchstone (1984). With an expanding portfolio, the studio produced movies as diverse as David Lynch's *Straight Story* (1999) and Gore Verbinski's *Pirates of the Caribbean* (2003) and television from the puppeteer Jim Henson's *The Muppets* to the teen comedy *High School Musical*. Appointed in 2005, CEO Bob Iger continued this trend, pushing Disney into new digital media. The corporation aggressively purchased competitor brands (such as Pixar in 2006) and major entertainment franchises (Marvel Comics in 2009 and Star Wars/Lucasfilm in 2012).

Disney also expanded its recreation business. In 1994, the company introduced its Disney Cruise Line range. With a fleet of cruise ships and one $850 million Haitian resort, the studio appeared capable of forging its own empire of tourism. Talk of the "Disney difference" in quality and "Disney magic" onboard situated the Disney cruise as a step above the standard experience.

Twenty-first-century Disney seemed capable of redefin-
ing expectations around leisure and recreation and of Disneyfying our free time. With its myriad parks, cruises, and
hotels, the company offered customers a real-life version
of the ride It's a Small World. In 2014 alone, the parks and
resorts wing made a profit of $2.6 billion, with four out
of five of the most successful theme parks in the United
States owned by the Burbank company.

The strategy of expansion into new forms of media
and recreation proved highly effective. Today the reality
is that everyone is a Disney consumer and that everyone has been Disneyfied. From Disneybaby channels to
Disney *Star Wars*, the corporation entertains the masses.
Through myriad advertising, television channels, and
product lines, the studio dominates family time. It caters
to all kinds of age groups. The extent of its reach is staggering. Children are now "born Disney." In 2011, the Disney Baby Initiative entailed studio representatives visiting
580 maternity hospitals across the United States to promote the brand. Andy Mooney, the chairman of Disney
Consumer Products Worldwide and responsible for the
Disney Princess brand, explained how with Disney Baby
he hoped "to develop a direct connection with first-time
moms," with the "lifetime value of connecting with new
families [being] perhaps more valuable to Disney than
any other brand." This desire to "win an infant" through

aggressive marketing represented both a generous help to mothers and a clever indoctrination program. Within nine months, the official "Disney Baby" Facebook community garnered 363,000 likes.

Seeking lucrative new markets, the Burbank studio targeted the richest echelons of society with the most expensive of goods. In 2015, Drew Harwell for the *Washington Post* accused the corporation of leaving behind its traditional middle-class market in its pursuit of revenue. With its US park division charging three-figure entry fees for the first time, Disney represented a "once in a lifetime" experience due to ticket costs more than anything else. "For America's middle-income vacationers, the Mickey Mouse Club, long promoted as 'made for you and me,' seems increasingly made for someone else," challenged the *Post*. That "someone else" appeared to be the top 10 percent earner. "Catering for Wall Street Dads" (and moms), the company redirected attention to luxury lagoon condos, à la carte cuisine, $1,200 Mickey Mouse bracelets on Fifth Avenue, and $4,595 Cinderella slippers designed by Jimmy Choo. Clearly at that price, not everyone could go to the ball. Purchase power dictated park access and enjoyment levels. Rather than bringing the nation together, Disney highlighted the economic divide. Where once "the nickel empire" of Coney Island catered to the masses, Disneyland had shifted its target from the middle class to business elite. With the title "Disney Hates Poor People," the roller-coaster community discussed whether the company had shifted strategy. Corporate profit motive threatened classic Disney social idealism.

Twenty-first-century expansion, the purchasing of competitor brands, and the shift away from a middle-class core highlighted weaknesses in the Disney fold. The purchase of Pixar, widely considered the most innovative producer of film animation and a long-term partner of Disney, highlighted how much the Burbank studio had lost its way. Compared to Pixar's succession of hits from *Toy Story* (1995) to *Finding Nemo* (2003), Disney productions lacked creativity and adult appeal. Arguably, in order to survive and prosper, Disney had shifted tactics to focus on the assimilation of other companies, without tackling its internal woes.

The procurement of Marvel and *Star Wars*, franchises with significant cultural presence, met with mixed response. Fans worried over the Disneyfication of much-loved American stories and their imminent demise into cartoon mediocrity. Once the great defender of American culture, the Walt Disney Company now threatened to dilute other notable cultural institutions. Mickey Mouse put Captain America in jeopardy and even endangered "the Force."

Initial fears proved misplaced. Disney oversaw production of a catalogue of acclaimed and commercially successful Marvel movies, taking advantage of a highly interactive Marvel multiverse to forge an expansive and highly cohesive filmic vision. With a track record of preserving its own authentic "magical kingdom" populated by Disney characters, the corporation tackled another "imaginary world" (or paracosm) with remarkable skill. Disney resurrected Stan Lee's 1960's The Avengers and lesser-known characters such as Ant-Man and made Marvel a mainstream property like never before.

Despite the corporation's success with superheroes, anxiety still ran high with a Disneyfied *Star Wars*. Concern over the impact of studio executives on the making of a new *Star Wars* movie spiraled, with the director J. J. Abrams reassuring fans that "they're not trying to Disney-fy it" (Grazer). Released in December 2015, *Star Wars: The Force Awakens* met with largely positive reviews. Content with a skilled retread of the original movie, filmgoers welcomed a revisit to a remarkably authentic 1970s *Star Wars* universe, with neither Mickey Mouse nor Jar Jar Binks in sight. Disneyfication seemed limited to an even-larger merchandising campaign than the original (the toymaker Keller's range of *Star Wars* figures in the late 1970s revolutionized the film-toy market) as well as plans for extending the franchise past its original arc of nine movies.

With two giant franchises subsumed, the growing Disneyfication of American popular culture seemed unstoppable. In late 2015, Disney revealed a total of eleven Marvel and six *Star Wars* movies ahead. In fact, there seemed far more science-fiction and comic-book titles on the horizon than original Disney-animated content. The new dominance of the Marvel and *Star Wars* worlds could also be witnessed at Anaheim's Disneyland. Formerly a Disneyesque vision of future technology, the Innoventions site at Tomorrowland closed to become the Expo Center, brimming with Marvel and *Star Wars* exhibits. Imagineers rebranded Space Mountain as Hyperspace Mountain. The new Galactic Grill sold sci-fi-themed food, including the Han burger and the pastry menace. A *Star Wars* theme overlaid the park. As the technology journalist Robin Burks remarked, "Here, the force hasn't just awakened, it's taken over the happiest place on Earth." The fifty-year-old *Star Wars* Padawan apprentice threatened to overwhelm its one-hundred-year-old adopted master. Rather than the Disneyfying of *Star Wars*, the *Star Wars*–izing of Disney seemed all the more in evidence. Ultimately, the long-term viability of Disneyfying rested in both corporate expansion and effective corporate assimilation. With *Star Wars*, Disney took on what may yet prove a "Force too strong with this one."

MERCHANDISING

Disney dollars are built around not just movies but merchandise. The studio story is a tale of successful product merchandising. Financial troubles plagued Walt Disney in his early decades. In his desire to keep his studio operational and popularize his staple characters, Walt welcomed corporate sponsorship and licensing. In 1929, he authorized a writing tablet adorned with the Mickey Mouse logo: the first Disney cartoon tie-in. In December of the same year, Walt formed Disney Enterprises to promote in-house merchandise.

In the 1930s, Mickey Mouse products included handkerchiefs, toffee, cereal boxes, train sets, and watches. The success of Mickey Mouse as a consumer product helped stave off collapse for a number of companies caught in the Great Depression. On the brink of bankruptcy, Ingersoll launched its first character watch, based on Mickey Mouse, in 1933. By 1935, Ingersoll had sold 2.5 million Mickey Mouse timepieces. The studio proved far from unique in embracing movie-merchandise opportunities. Alongside *Snow White* soundtracks, consumers picked up Judy Garland dolls tied to the release of MGM's *The Wizard of Oz* (1939).

However, only Disney realized the true merit of merchandise to its business model and consistently experimented with license ideas. With the advent of World War II, the Disney war effort included not only propaganda films but Mickey Mouse gas masks for kids. Under license, the Sun Rubber Company produced around one thousand rodent-themed masks designed to alleviate child wartime anxiety while preparing them for the possibility of unexpected attack. The headgear put Mickey Mouse on the front line in the defense against chemical warfare. In the 1950s, the studio's *Davy Crockett* television series led to the sale of ten million Crockett coonskin hats, along with many more replica rifles. In 1987, the first Disney Store opened in Glendale Galleria in Glendale, California. Promising a magical experience for guests, the store sold only official Disney merchandise. The model rolled out to markets across North America, Europe, and the Far East. In recent years, the studio has put *Frozen* and *Star Wars* imagery on almost every product imaginable, from Olaf the Snowman snow globes to Chewbacca pajamas. Disney Culture increasingly resembles an assembly line of plastic toys, with the commercial aim of total market saturation.

The appeal of such merchandise is based around a number of themes. On a basic level, people buy Disney products to keep their children (or themselves) happy. The company cleverly ties consumption with its own "happiness" ethos. Official Disney products are typically good quality and lavishly presented. They are family friendly and child safe. People buy because the products are American and tell good old-fashioned American stories. They buy out of compulsion, addiction, and as dutiful servants of an ever-expanding consumer culture. Fans immerse themselves in the world of Disneyana.

Parks encourage the collecting bug by selling thousands of badges, coins, and soft toys. Disney officially introduced "pin trading" into its parks in 1999. Pin variants now exceed sixty thousand, with rare pins (containing tiny remnants of props and rides) reselling for hundreds of dollars. The company sought to control the pin market by introducing strict trading rules governing cast members' lanyards and even the touching of others' pins. In 2002, Tokyo Disneyland banned "pinswaps" due to traders and their mats taking over the park. The pins serve as symbols of emotional attachment to the studio. They highlight the commercial devotion of fans to the Disney brand. The corporation meanwhile tightly controls its product lines by carefully timing limited editions, rereleases, and licensing. Sometimes, maintaining brand and image leads to controversy, as when the studio threatened to sue three South Florida day-care centers for unlicensed use of its characters in 1989. The Disney adage "you don't mess with the mouse" applies to all and sundry.

THEMING

Alongside merchandizing, theming remains a crucial aspect to the Walt Disney Company's success. The company has perfected themed capitalism. Theme parks operate as cleverly disguised commercial lands. The opening of Disneyland in 1955 represented a triumph of imaginative capitalism. While promoted as a revolutionary family adventure, Disneyland very much pandered to consumer tastes of the period. With a nod to the new craze of purpose-built shopping complexes, Main Street USA functioned as one giant shopping mall. The company's 1953 prospectus introduced the concept of Main Street as "the main shopping district of Disneyland," with its centerpiece a Disney Emporium "where you can buy almost anything and everything unusual" (WED Enterprises). Visitors to the Emporium would find "magnificently plumed birds and fantastic fish from all over the world, and which may be purchased and shipped anywhere in the US if you so desire." The final version of Main Street featured a cigar store, a bank, and the adult-apparel store Hollywood Maxwell, with a display titled "The Wizard of Bras."

Opening stores linked with individual films, Disneyland helped popularize "themed shopping." Corporate-sponsored attractions included the Monsanto Hall of Chemistry and Kaiser Aluminum Land, the latter offering visitors a "delightfully true told story of how the sleeping giant of metals—aluminum—was awakened and has become your friendly servant" (Martens). Visitors then met the industrial mascot KAP the pig. The studio coupled rides with stores selling mementos of the experience. Seamless transition blurred the divides between recreation and commerce. Visitors came to comprehend the theme park in consumer-based terms: navigating pathways by what they could eat and what they could purchase. The park experience rested on buying goods rather than on enjoying thrill rides. Stores sold basically the same products but with different character and ride skins, granting the illusion of difference. Entertainment meant consumption rather than recreation. Disney altered the meaning of the modern amusement park to rest on its qualities as first and foremost a consumer experience.

With a focus on providing an immersive themed experience for visitors, California's Disneyland emerged as a conceptual twin to Nevada's Las Vegas in the 1950s. The rise of themed casinos such as the Frontier in Vegas spurred such comparison. In 1958, Julian Halevy compared the two booming entertainment capitals of the West, their fantasy realms fulfilling "a growing need in the United States to escape from reality," as well as their common desire to extort high dollar expenditure. Halevy derided the "mumbo-jumbo," "gimmicks," and "feeble sham" of Disneyland and ultimately preferred how Vegas more openly and brazenly "deals in the essence of the American way, narcoticizes the number-one preoccupation of daily reality and nightly dream: the Almighty Buck." Both Disneyland and Vegas captured a new idolatry around the dollar. Colorful and hyperreal commercial landscapes, Disneyland and Las Vegas attracted great interest. Populated with animatronic figures and fairground machines, Disneyland seemed little different from casino halls of one-armed bandits at Vegas. As themed shrines to entertainment capitalism, both Vegas and Disney promoted a fantasy of riches and demanded healthy contributions to enter the church. Visitors felt bombarded at both landscapes by the wealth of simulation, stimulation, and expenditure opportunities. While Vegas mostly focused on adult entertainment in the 1950s, Disney targeted the whole family. By the 1990s, the two landscapes had grown closer together. With colorful to-scale replications of Paris and Venice, as well as fun stores such as M&Ms and the cartoonish Excalibur hotel, sin city looked increasingly Disneyfied. Local boosters had no qualms exploding old casinos and creating new themed luxury hotels. The same boom-and-bust mentality led to a shifting roster of rides at Anaheim. Disneyland and Las Vegas reinvented themselves to attract new clientele.

Disneyland and Las Vegas also promoted themed experiences based around convergence. As Henry Jenkins explains, "In the world of media convergence, every important story gets told, every brand gets sold, and every consumer gets courted across multiple media platforms" (3). Disney first experimented with convergence in the 1950s, advertising its wares on the television program *Disneyland* for ABC that in turn financed the park. The studio realized that different media, advertising, and consumer paths could be brought together and that convergence encouraged more consumption and brand loyalty. The company's ability to move stories across media platforms has since proved exceptional. At Disneyland, visitors move from queue to themed ride to themed shop to themed eatery in one seamless act, all based around a story. For Alan Bryman, this represents a process of "dedifferentiation of consumption" or "hybrid consumption," whereby traditional boundaries between consumer activities collapse within the fantasy worlds of Disney (viii). Disney Stores arguably resemble miniature Disneylands, or vice versa. The Pirates of the Caribbean ride led to a hugely successful movie franchise that in turn led to videogames and Jack Sparrow books. Outside Disney, the trend can be seen in malls that resemble theme parks (for example the Mall of America in Bloomington, Minnesota, with its own roller coaster) and theme parks that resemble malls. This new liminality in consumer life marks important shifts in society. Stories are now based on toys and games, and toys based on stories. Origin points and nativity arguably no longer matter.

Only on occasion has Disney's dependence on themed commerce let it down. One notable example is Disney's California Adventure. First mooted at a summer retreat in Aspen in 1995, California Adventure represented an ambitious attempt to expand business in the Los Angeles region. Envisaged as a "cheap" idea ($650 million estimate, actual cost around $1 billion), the park concept promised accurate reproductions of Californian monuments and a more adult feel than Disneyland, located opposite. Over three years, Disney Imagineers transformed a seventy-two-acre site, formerly a parking lot, into a newly themed world. Like Anaheim's orange groves giving way to Disneyland's Sleeping Beauty Castle, asphalt disappeared to give rise to a simulated California. California Adventure opened February 8, 2001, and Roy E. Disney, Mickey Mouse, and Michael Eisner stood before giant "CALIFORNIA" letters and a replica of the Golden Gate Bridge, welcoming in the dedication "all who believe in the power of dreams" (Disney and Eisner).

The cartoonish theming of California proved a huge disappointment. Visitors complained about the lackluster parades, smoke billowing from the evening pyrotechnic show, the dearth of attractions (a total of twenty-three counting a bread-baking demo and a tortilla-making exhibit), and the absence of children's activities. The high-end restaurants by the chef Wolfgang Puck and the wine promoter Robert Mondavi quickly disappeared from the park, while the McDonald's Hamburger spaceship, in all its Happy Meal glory, remained. Brook Barnes for the *New York Times* reported how for most guests the park proved a "colossal disappointment" ("Disney Looking"). Even CEO Bob Iger called it "a brand eyesore" (Barnes, "Disney Looking").

Two key problems of themed commerce emerged within the park. First, the park was not very *Disney*. It sported few staple characters or themes. A re-creation of a 1920s amusement park, Paradise Pier, for example, resembled Coney Island more than a Mickey Mouse cartoon. The purchase of standardized rides, rather than bespoke Disney ones, solidified the generic image. Brady MacDonald for the *Los Angeles Times* described the "on-the-cheap, off-the-shelf nature" of the park ("Disney California Adventure: A Peek"). Gary Warner for the *Orange County*

Register suggested, "I'm not a Disney Imagineer, but how about some great rides tied to *The Lion King, Pocahontas, Hercules, Aladdin,* or *The Little Mermaid*?" Disney seemed to have forgotten how to Disneyfy itself.

Second, the park failed as a re-creation of California. It presented the Golden State as an elongated shopping trip, vacuous and identityless: a decidedly empty experience. It was also superfluous. Across the walkway, Disneyland already epitomized the theme-park West by its frontierism, film sets, and decidedly Californian sympathies, while farther out lay Universal Studios and the real Hollywood. Visitors already had plenty of "California experience" in California. The park felt like a Disney tourist attraction based on tourist attractions, a movie-set version of a much-filmed state, or an uninspired simulation of existing simulations.

Between 2007 and 2012, Disney renovated the park at a cost of $1.1 billion, adding new rides, retheming old ones, highlighting the history of California, and adding two new lands (Cars Land and Buena Vista Street). Iger simply called the quest to add "Disney DNA" (Barnes, "Revamped Disney Park"). The Hollywood-style makeover featured a number of obvious cosmetic changes, with Mickey Mouse added to the giant Ferris wheel and the surprising deletion of the California letters. A new $80 million fountain show with twelve hundred jets of water proved a Disney rival to the fountains of Versailles. An interpretation of Walt's arrival in 1920s Los Angeles, Buena Vista Street boasted incredible historical details, from a replica of the Pan Pacific Auditorium to temporally accurate drain signage and streetcar advertising. The park showed Disney history at its best: architectural, artistic, and colorful. Cars Land paid homage to Route 66 kitsch and highlighted the company's ability to package nostalgia. It also spoke of the studio's creative reliance on Pixar. The facelift partially worked. One economic analyst enthused, "The park has been fully transformed from a random collection of a couple of great rides into a true Disney-worthy themed world" (Barnes, "Revamped Disney Park"). Others proved less enthusiastic. Writing in 2012, Brady MacDonald felt that California Adventure 2.0 "still probably needs another billion dollars in improvements before it can be worthy of the Disney name" ("Disney California Adventure: How We Got Here"). In 2014, attendance increased to 8.7 million but fell considerably short of crowds gathering at the park opposite.

MCDISNEY

Given the Walt Disney Company's distinctive image and history, it is all too easy to exceptionalize the corporation. However, it shares much in common with other major twentieth-century US companies. Disney's huge successes in the 1950s happened at the same time as the beginning of that American staple Walmart (1962) and the opening of the first franchised outlets of Kentucky Fried Chicken (1952) and McDonald's (1955). The fast-food giant McDonald's in particular makes for good comparison with Disney. The project of Richard and Maurice McDonald, the first McDonald's opened in San Bernardino in 1940. In 1955, the same year as Disneyland opened, McDonald's became a franchise corporation under the stewardship of new investor, Ray Kroc. Kroc served with Walt Disney in World War I. Kroc and Disney held similarly conservative values. The first McDonald's restaurant and the first Disney park sit only a few miles apart. Kroc even approached Disney about gaining a concession inside.

The two businesses work by similar rational, systematic processes and boast a very similar work culture. In the 1990s, the sociologist George Ritzer, working on McDonald's, identified the principles of control, efficiency, calculability, and predictability to lie at the heart of the Big Mac's success. People wanted standardized, cheap, but sizable burgers that they could eat quickly. Ritzer argued that the McDonald's system of work (which he labeled "McDonaldization") applied to all kinds of industries. As he observed, "the principles of the fast-food restaurant are coming to dominate more and more sectors of American society as well as of the rest of the world" (1). McDonaldization could be seen in the fast-food sector, retail, universities, and prisons.

Disney might be taken as another McDonaldized corporation: one that prides itself on efficiency, organization, consumer experience, and control. Like McDonald's, the studio rigorously trains its staff in work culture. McDonald's offers the McDucktorate to its best students, while Disney University offers the Disney College Program. Both corporations serve as business models for other companies to emulate. From 2000, the Disney Institute has sold "business excellence" courses to myriad corporations, preaching the "universal pillars of a successful business—leadership, culture, service, brand, and innovation" through Disney-specific examples. Unofficial books on the "Disney way" raise the caliber of other corporations by them "harnessing the management secrets of Disney in your company" (Capodagli and Jackson). As Alan Bryman highlights, the "Disney way" is not just for Disneyphiles. Many corporations have been both Disneyized and McDonaldized.

For scholars such as Ritzer, it is McDonald's, with its thousands of fast-food outlets around the world, rather than Disney, that serves as a "more powerful symbol and force in our age" (136). However, if we take into account

Disney's more wholesome (and healthy) image projected by modern media into almost every home, the influence ratio dramatically changes. Perhaps rather than the two organizations being in competition, both Disney and McDonald's speak to a broader revival of Fordism in the twentieth century and a resurgence of fondness for order and predictability in anxious times. Both institutions have successfully weathered change and adapted their business models, including "localizing" products. Both McDonald's culture and Disney Culture have developed over time. Both are known for their mascots and their sloganeering (from "Have a Nice Day" to the "Disney smile"). Both conspicuously target the child as consumer, through Happy Meals and Disney toys. Certainly, Disney and McDonald's have much in common.

DISNEY AND THE TRIUMPH OF CONSUMER CAPITALISM

The success of Disney also highlights the triumph of consumer capitalism in the modern age. The plastic spires of the Magic Kingdom castle demark an icon of European elitism remodeled as a childish whimsy for purchase. Disneyland functions as a shrine to modern capitalism. It provides a utopic and irresistible consumer landscape for its guests. Behind the mouse lies immense corporate power and business acumen. Cartoon characters serve as a pencil-thin veil for shrewd and expansive capital operations. Caught up in Disney folklore and simulation, people forget the money behind the mouse. When the pop celebrity Will.i.am claimed, "Harrods is like Disneyland for shoppers," he failed to recognize Disneyland itself as the ultimate consumer playground, more a constant conveyor belt of goods than rides.

The advance of Disney Culture reflects a fundamental shift toward a consumer-based way of life. Fjellman declares how "the world we live in is a world of commodities" (7). With around two hundred stores selling official merchandise, Florida's Walt Disney World is an example par excellence. Disney has contributed to the commodification of life, leisure, and narrative. Leftist scholars have targeted the studio for precisely this turn. Identifying Disney as the home of cultural blandness and mundane excess, Giroux decries the wider "corporate domination of public culture" (28). Disney is part of a "culture industry" described by Max Horkheimer and Theodor Adorno as where factories produce goods for the masses that fulfill false psychological needs (like "living like a Disney princess") while rendering people passive consumers bereft of their own imagination. Horkheimer and Adorno contended that "culture today is infecting everything with sameness" (94), and for them, Donald Duck cartoons spelled "the breaking of all individual resistance" (110). As Halevy wrote of Disneyland in the 1950s, "the whole world, the universe, and all man's striving for dominion over self and nature, have been reduced to a sickening blend of cheap formulas designed to sell."

Criticism aside, American culture increasingly derives from consumer-based values. Commerce shapes the form and flow of popular trends. Disney Culture is part of this transition. The Walt Disney Company serviced a decisive consumer turn in the twentieth century. It popularized the unison of fantasy, media, and mass consumption. Walt's personal vision of utopia facilitated the rise of entertainment capital. The French Marxist Guy Debord details a process whereby "an obvious downgrading of *being* into *having*" encouraged "a generalized shift from *having* to appearing" (17) that ultimately leads to the "historical moment at which the commodity completes its colonization of social life" (42). Disney is part of such a historical denouement: the victory of consumption over culture. The reality is that we are all invested in the mouse.

PROTESTING THE CORPORATE MOUSE

As an enduring symbol of American capitalism, the Walt Disney Company has proved a popular target for criticism and protest. Alongside McDonald's, Coca-Cola, and Starbucks, the studio remains a staple of anticapitalist and anti-American propaganda and rallies. Critics have denounced it as anodyne, superficial, childish, profiteering, and bland. Mickey Mouse has been attacked, defiled, and even destroyed. The postmodern theorist Jean Baudrillard vilified Disney Culture as ruinous, declaring, "The whole Walt Disney philosophy eats out of your hand with these pretty little sentimental creatures in grey fur coats. For my own part, I believe that behind these smiling eyes there lurks a cold, ferocious beast fearfully stalking us" (*America* 48). Artistic criticism includes the sculpture *Twentieth Century War Memorial*, featuring a rotting Mickey Mouse and a machine gun, by Michael Sandle and *Mickey Mouse at the Front* by the Gulf War artist John Keane. Online, the videogame Los Disneys attacks the Disney universe by coupling a Doom-type first-person shooter with a visit to a virtual Disneyland. Los Disneys offers a perverted postapocalyptic Disneyland for players to traverse, rife with lethal children and scary animatronics. The videogame fiction recounts Michael Eisner's plans to unleash doomsday, with Walt cast as a cryogenically preserved Anti-Christ.

In August 2015, the British artist and social critic Banksy erected "Dismaland Bemusement Park" at the former public swimming pool in Weston-super-Mare, a dilapidated town along the English coast. Open to all but "legal representatives of the Walt Disney Corporation" for a limited five-week period, Dismaland functioned as a theme park, political statement, and unorthodox art gallery for a range of mostly British and American artists. While Banksy denied "an issue with Disney" and offered *Frozen*'s "Let It Go" as "pure gold," his project nonetheless amounted to a sophisticated parody of the Disney brand (E. Mills). Sporting a Banksy version of the Disney logo and advertised as a new take on "the happiest place on earth," Dismaland turned traditional Disney staples into symbols of the disaffected and disenfranchised.

Dismaland inverted the fairy tale of cartoon princesses and "happily ever after" to present a far more troubling narrative of death and decay: more global nightmare than American Dream. Like Warhol's "Myths," Dismaland functioned as satire art of Disney Culture. Inside the concrete makeshift berms of the park, Mickey Mouse–eared staff provided decidedly "dismal" service by throwing guidebooks at visitors, crumpling tickets, and blocking photographs. A stern sneer replaced the Disney smile, and a pretend dislike usurped "have a nice day." Some staff pointed replica rifles at visitors, while others sabotaged amusement-park games. Their high jinks highlighted the typical problems of theme parks and Disney Culture: high prices, fake smiles, and banal experiences.

Meanwhile, the icons of Disney were reengineered for a darker world. Visitors discovered a sculpture of Mickey Mouse transformed into a deadly snake and Minnie Mouse on a torn billboard above an apocalyptic landscape. At the ground zero of the park, a tarnished, postindustrial mimic of Disney's Cinderella Castle captured the gaze of spectators and gave the park its focal identity. Inside the castle, a Disneyfied re-creation of the paparazzi-fueled car crash in which Princess Diana died, complete with overturned pink carriage, drew guests to take their own snapshots of the carnage. Banksy employed Disney as cipher to comment on a wide range of topics from terrorism and immigration to good parenting and community responsibility. Dismaland connected the Burbank studio to social and environmental decay. To a degree, Banksy took on the role of Disneyfying the undesirable, the real, the radical—the realms that the Walt Disney Company itself traditionally left well outside its parks. As the artist explained, "We just built a family attraction that acknowledges inequality and impending catastrophe. I would argue it's theme parks which ignore these things that are the twisted ones." Rather than an escape to a "better" world, Dismaland offered a hard-hitting reminder of the real one. Meanwhile, that Banksy succeeded with his own coherent, signature version of Disneyland proved that his work, at least in Britain, had become as much a "recognizable label" as Walt Disney. Dismaland showed the Banksyfication of Disney and hinted at an ironic, postapocalyptic, post-Disney world.

4

DISNEY VALUES

In 2013, Disney released the animated story of two princesses, Anna and Elsa, coming to terms with their emotions and powers in a magical ice kingdom. The movie *Frozen* became a box-office sensation, so successful that media spoke of *Frozen* fever and the *Frozen* phenomenon. From sippy cups to karaoke booths to ice shows, the movie seemed everywhere. Children watched the film so many times that parents feared addiction issues, children being unable to "let it go."

For almost a century, Disney has played a formative role in American culture. Generations have grown up with the studio's creations. Disney Culture has shaped American mass culture by dominating family entertainment and recreation. The company has promoted a range of fundamental notions and ideals through its movies: universal love, good conquering evil, and simple happy endings. It has also pushed a range of cultural and social values: a Protestant-style work ethic, absolute morality, and traditional family roles. Chris Rojek contends that Disney pursues a code of "moral regulation" (122) over its audience, in a sense keeping people in line with Walt's conservative vision, while others argue that the studio oversimplifies life and social situations with its "Mickey Mouse morality." In the case of *Frozen*, scriptwriters both rallied to traditional notions of family (for example, sisterly love) and forwarded notions of rebellion. Assuming that the Walt Disney Company is consistent in its social values may prove a fallacy. What is certain is that the Burbank studio has influenced popular views of family, gender, race, and the environment over the past century and continues to exert a powerful hold over today's audiences. Disney Culture clearly has an effect on society.

THE DISNEY CHILD

For Walt Disney, childhood represented a realm of innocence and simplicity. Cartoons reconnected him with the romantic spirit of youth. Disney Culture is fundamentally a culture of childhood. Cartoons offer a childlike gaze on the world and, in turn, influence how children navigate their own experiences. Disney channels, stores, toys, films, and games introduce kids to Disney ideas, concepts, characters, and values. Movies such as *The Lion King* and *Frozen* are part of the Disneyfication of childhood.

Often a trusted extension of the family, the Walt Disney Company educates kids in how to behave and what is good and bad about society. It teaches a moral code, where good always conquers evil. Children learn by Disney, repeating songs, humming tunes, sometimes spending more time with Walt's characters than with their parents. The studio invaluably introduces children to a "larger world" outside their home, showing them new animals and environments. Disney movies have introduced children to such adult themes as melancholia, loss, violence, and death. The corporation thus exercises tremendous influence over childhood imagination, behavior, and values. As the media professor Lee Artz claims, "Disney has replaced schools, churches, and families in teaching society right and wrong" (122). Critics argue that this Mickey Mouse monopoly over childhood limits imagination and free play and that children grow up Disneyfied.

The studio also promotes the "inner child" in adults. The corporation has continually celebrated the phenomenon of "not growing up." About *Snow White*, Walt Disney explained, "I didn't make the picture for children. I made it for adults—for the child that exists in all adults" (Barrier 131). Similarly, he remained adamant that "Disneyland isn't designed just for children. When does a person stop being a child? Can you say that a child is ever entirely eliminated from an adult?" (Thomas ix). The story of a boy who never grows up, the studio's *Peter Pan* attested to such thought. Disney Culture contributed to a broader psychological shift in the twentieth century toward celebrating the "inner child." The company's dedication to eternal youth complemented the rise of the "me" generation and adults playing kid games. Disney Culture has helped all ages enjoy cartoons and animation with less judgment.

LIVING DISNEY: DISNEY AS SOCIAL EXPERIMENT

One of Walt Disney's grand dreams was to create a "future city" where everyone could live harmoniously. Although Walt died too early to witness his vision realized, a number of "living Disney" projects have incorporated his ideas. From Celebration to EPCOT, Disney Culture features a variety of real-world outlets. Disney Culture has at its most extreme and purest reflection encouraged people to "be" Disney on a day-to-day level.

At twenty-five thousand acres in size, considerably larger than Manhattan, Walt Disney World (WDW), Florida, is one example of living Disney. WDW features four parks, 140 attractions, thirty-six hotels, a power plant, a private security force, and laundry facilities for thirty thousand staff. As Austin Carr maintains, "Disney World isn't an amusement park. It's a metropolis." At the very least, WDW is akin to a giant gated community sporting white middle-class values. Inside WDW lies EPCOT, an experimental prototype world first imagined by Walt that showcases the Disney community perfected. As Rojek contends, WDW functions as a "living advertisement for Disney Culture" (129).

In 1996, Disney opened its first town, Celebration, to residents in Florida, just five miles south of WDW. In many regards, Celebration represented the epitome of "living Disney" and the apogee of Disney Culture. Residents of Celebration lived, breathed, and slept Disney. As eleven thousand residents moved into their homes, a new urban planning project unfolded. Celebration embodied the ultimate Disney Culture experiment—a town designed, styled, and revolving around Walt Disney. The studio allied itself with a mix of new urbanism and traditional family values. Celebration paid homage to old suburban towns such as Lakewood and Levittown but updated the design template to include high technology and surveillance. The corporation built porches to encourage neighborliness and provided communal spaces for social activities. Celebration appeared the perfect embodiment of the classic American Dream.

Disney Culture at Celebration also entailed a level of control. Town dictates determined paint colors, parking limits, and garden foliage (with lawns limited to two inches of growth). The studio assumed authority over the town's decisions. Demographics revealed a predictably white middle-class dominance (88 percent in the 2000 census). For critics, Celebration appeared a bastardized or Disneyfied re-creation of the *Stepford Wives*, a province of insipid fakery populated by Hannah Montana wanna-bees, with the innate feeling of being trapped inside *The Truman Show*. With Celebration's Disney-style fantasy architecture and artificial snow at Christmas, the "town" (technically an unincorporated community) offended the culture elite. It also failed to meet the Disney claim of being "the happiest place on earth." Preaching such lofty goals, Celebration came under closer scrutiny than other planned communities. Economic recession, along with a suicide and a murder in 2010, tarnished the utopic image. Tamara Lush at the *Huffington Post* reveled in the irony of how residents "woke up . . . to the sight of yellow crime-scene tape wrapped around a condo near the Christmas-decorated downtown, where Bing Crosby croons from speakers hidden in the foliage." Another newspaper headlined, "How the Disney Dream Died in Celebration" (Pilkington). Disney's utopian experiment joined other corporate-inspired communities such as Fordlandia and Oldsmar, Florida.

While Celebration proved less of a success than Disney expected, the company continued to dabble in urban living schemes. As part of the growing WDW project, the studio opened the "resort community" of Golden Oak inside the park in 2013. Golden Oak represented a scaled-down Celebration for the rich, a Disney-themed gated community. Corporate advertising depicted beaming dads with Mickey Mouse ears and their young "Disney princesses" spending magical days at home and inside the park. In fact, the home and parkscape blended, with no hint of berms or buffer zones. Golden Oak promised a "lifetime of Disney traditions of every sort" and a total Disney lifestyle experience (Walt Disney Company, "Welcome"). High-tech custom homes came with use of the private clubhouse and a concierge service to the rides. The opportunity to "live the Disney dream" and reside in a fantasyland of permanent Disney smiles carried a hefty surcharge: the price of immersing yourself permanently in the fantasy of Walt Disney and the "happily ever afters" started from $2 million. While most Americans could buy into studio whimsy at their local K-Mart, only the very few could afford to live designer twenty-four-hour Disney Culture. With Golden Oak, the company targeted a very niche audience: cash-rich Mickey Mouse obsessives. As with designer Mickey Mouse jewelry and VIP experiences, Disney's market reached out to the powerful American businessperson.

For even the most dedicated of fans, procuring a property in WDW represented an unattainable wish upon a star. Instead, Disneyphiles employed other means to fuel their fantasies and embrace Disney Culture. Repetitious watching of animated movies and hours spent on Disney videogames facilitated immersion. Die-hard veterans festooned in pins and badges roamed Disney parks. With a wealth of official products available, people consumed Disney, and Disney consumed their homes. One collector, known simply as "Disney Claire," amassed around thirty thousand items by 2014, her emotional attachment to the brand described as "like a drug." Her home served as both a personal shrine and a cluttered museum to Walt Disney, although her husband failed to muster the requisite Disney smile, confessing, "sleeping in a Little Mermaid bed doesn't sort of fill me with a great deal of joy."

Other Disneyphiles created "Disney bucket lists" of recreational experiences, including marriage at the WDW wedding pavilion and riding with the conductor on the Disneyland railroad. Dining at Club 33, an exclusive restaurant at Disneyland open to a small, rich, and elite crowd, with membership dues of around $27,000

per annum, proved another status symbol. The artist
Marthe A. Andersen labeled such fandom "obsessive
Disney disorder" (O.D.D.), a fictitious illness. The Walt
Disney Company helped indulge its clientele. Its annual
D23 Expo, a Disneyfied comic-con where princesses and
cartoons ruled, garnered huge crowds eager to witness
new products. Within the fan fraternity, loyalists known
as Pixie Dusters saw their role as defending the studio to
the hilt and dubbed any criticism heresy. For some, the
obsession goes just too far. In July 2015, Orange County
sheriffs apprehended Jerry Moody, a homeless man who
for ten years had routinely visited Disneyland and not
paid for any of his food. The serial "dine and dasher" justi-
fied himself by simply admitting that he "likes to come to
Disney" (S. Allen).

THE DISNEY FAN: DISNEY AS ALTERNATIVE RELIGION

In a 1934 article titled "Mickey and Minnie," the author
E. M. Forster declared, "Mickey is everybody's God."
The appeal of the studio is remarkable. Fans buy into
the fantasy world in a way resembling spiritual devotion.
They worship the brand as if it is an alternative religion.
Disciples sport the couture of the mouse and maintain
a naïve but cultish affinity with all that Mickey conjures.
Disney World and Cinderella Castle resemble pilgrimage

sites akin to Jerusalem or Mecca. For the scholar Richard Foglesong, Disneyland is the "Vatican with Mouse Ears" (24). For some people, Disney is the closest they get to a modern religious experience.

The studio keenly supports such adoration. Active in self-mythology, it venerates Mickey and Walt as untouchable demigods. The Disney Institute encourages employees to see how Disney Culture depends on the "presence of deep attachment to the brand, not simply the presence of repeated purchase behavior." Richard Breaux of Colorado State University argues that "Disney films represent the powerful and positive attributes of magical thinking and prayer where prayer is answered and wishes and dreams come true" (401). A symptom of broader shifts in the past century away from organized religion and toward new forms of worship, Disney supports the transition to more individualized spiritualism. The studio offers people a kind of generic new religion built around consumerism and media, with hopes of the "happily ever after" and a place where dreams come true.

DISNATURE AND DISNEY ENVIRONMENTALISM

Disney has also helped foster a pronature philosophy and a welcome environmental sensibility among its viewers. Nature has proved fundamental to the spread of Disney

Culture, and more than any other company, Disney has consistently promoted a nature-friendly gaze. Disney is hardly Disney without Mickey Mouse, Donald Duck, Baloo the bear, Pumba the warthog, and Sebastian the crab. Raised on a farm, Walt Disney romanticized rural nature as full of animal characters. He studied the photographer Eadweard Muybridge on animal form and incorporated nature into his early animation. As the scholar David Whitley argues, "the theme of wild nature forms the very heartland of Disney's animated features" (1). Movies have reshaped "nature" into a decidedly Disney product: friendly, anthropomorphic, entertaining, harmless, innocent, fantastical, childish, reductive, and significantly under our (human) control. Nature has undergone a process of Disneyfication and come out as "Disnature," a cartoon version of the wild that is loved and adored by its audience (Wills 180).

The rise of Disnature is important as it corresponds with the fall of real nature in our lives. Tied to the demographic shift away from farms and toward the metropolis, the demise of daily interaction with the "great outdoors" left an experiential void in the twentieth century. National and state parks provided temporary bandages on the transition, but Disnature helped bring nature properly into the home. Disney fulfilled the human desire for contact with flora and fauna, albeit through a highly filtered conduit. Children began to know "nature" through a Disney lens.

As well as servicing a human need, the Burbank studio has promoted a long-term environmental perspective in its movies and documentaries. It has tackled a range of environmental concerns, including hunting, animal liberation, resource use, and global warming. Classic Disney animations including *Fox and the Hound*, *101 Dalmatians*, *Mary Poppins*, and *Bambi* have questioned the American hunting tradition. The controversial scene depicting the loss of Bambi's mother to sportsmen in the 1942 classic fueled a whole movement against hunters. The scholar Ralph Lutts has labeled the damage done by the studio to the American tradition "The Bambi Syndrome." Inspired by a short story for a children's storytelling device called the Roll-a-Book, Disney's *Dumbo* (1941) featured a range of archetypal Burbank elements: trains, circuses, and animal friendship. Through the prism of circus life, the movie commented on issues of animal imprisonment and animal rights. The studio has usually focused on "happiness" as its ethos but has shown itself capable of tackling emotional loss in an environmental domain. In the live-action film *Old Yeller* (1957), audiences watched its canine star be killed because of rabies. The nature documentary series *True-Life Adventures* (1948–60) and *DisneyNature* (2008–present) position Disney not just as a promoter of the natural world but as a key force in environmental education.

Released in 2008, the Disney/Pixar animated movie *Wall-E* highlighted a corporation keen to promote environmental awareness. The movie told the story of Wall-E, a garbage compressor that is stranded on postapocalyptic Earth and falls for an "extraterrestrial vegetation evaluator" (Eve). Joining a roster of environmental doomsday visions and "lost Earth" nostalgia pieces from Lars Von Trier's *Melancholia* (2011) to Hollywood's *The Day after Tomorrow* (2004) and *2012* (2009), Pixar's *Wall-E* grappled with environmental endings. Wall-E himself resembled a machine-tooled Robinson Crusoe caught up in an unfolding eco-drama. The movie proved a huge success. According to Brandon Keim of *Wired*, "The decade's most powerful environmental film doesn't star Al Gore or Greenpeace activists, but a trash-compacting, *Hello Dolly*–loving robot with a cockroach as a best friend." *New York Times* called it an "ecological parable" (Scott). *Wall-E* recycled old concepts (such as spaceships escaping a polluted Earth) but also offered some novel ideas about technology, machinery, and mass consumption. Radically, *Wall-E* offered consumer capitalism as the core problem resulting in ecocide. The environmentalist Jessica Jensen for the *Huffington Post* noted how "the scenes on the Axiom [spaceship] are scarily reminiscent of present-day Las Vegas: the over-fed humans are detached from their daily cares and are free to sit on their backsides, consume, and be constantly entertained." The entertainment-focused Axiom travelers equally resembled most movie attendees, as well as Disneyphiles on their own journeys to Disneyland.

Disney also promoted the environment in its parks. Opened on Earth Day April 22, 1998, Animal Kingdom at Walt Disney World attested to the studio's long-term eco-alliance. Casting the natural world as part drama, part education, Michael Eisner declared, "Welcome to a kingdom of animals . . . real, ancient, and imagined: a kingdom ruled by lions, dinosaurs, and dragons; a kingdom of balance, harmony and survival; a kingdom we enter to share in wonder, gaze at the beauty, thrill at the drama, and learn" (PR Newswire, "Disney's Animal Kingdom"). Disney Culture incorporated elaborate fantasies about nature past and present. Placed at the hub of the park, the towering Tree of Life, complete with its own nature-themed gift store, served as a wilderness equivalent of Disney World's Cinderella Castle. Consisting of several themed zones, the park encouraged visitors to embark on their own safari into Africa and jungle trek into Asia (as well as stop off at the Pizzafari in Discovery Land). The corporation explained, "Inspiring a love of animals and concern for their welfare is the underlying theme, both

subtle and obvious, throughout Disney's Animal Kingdom Park" (Tomkins).

Criticism of the corporation highlighted its mixed environmental record, its questionable educational reliability,
and its packaging of nature as a product. Along with concerns over deleterious effects on the Everglades with the
expansion of WDW, environmentalists drew attention to
the twenty-nine animal deaths prior to the Animal Kingdom opening. Arguably, the park operated as one huge
simulation of nature and one giant Disney nature store.
The park peddled antiquated notions of animal entertainment by offering safari-like colonial adventuring in the
style of Teddy Roosevelt the hunter. The artificial foliage
of the Disney Tree of Life attested to human mastery over
nature. With its ten thousand vinyl leaves and height of
145 feet, the Disney Tree of Life threatened to replace the
American redwood in popular celebration, with more
people heading to Disney parks than Yosemite. Disnature
also failed to translate into real activism. Inviting visitors
to "be a conservation hero" and "join us in supporting
efforts for wildlife around the world," the Animal Kingdom granted guests the illusion of saving nature, of being
the eco-hero and playing the conservationist inside park
berms (Walt Disney Company, "Animal Kingdom"). But
did the park ease the eco-conscience of visitors or moti-
vate them to protest outside? Arguably, Disney helped

fashion the "consumer environmentalist": one who sponsors exotic tigers and buys flat white lattes at Starbucks in Animal Kingdom because a percentage of proceeds go to the cotton-top tamarin.

DISNEY AND RACE

Critics also draw attention to how the company tackles race in society. Commentators accuse Walt Disney of racism and highlight the studio's use of stereotypes in a range of movies, citing the African American jive crows in *Dumbo*, the Asian American Siamese cats and Latino Chihuahuas in *The Lady and the Tramp* (1955) and heavily caricatured Native Americans in *Pocahontas*. In response to the Europeanized *Mulan* (1998), forty thousand people signed a petition complaining that Disney "whitewashed" its characters. From *Snow White* to *Frozen*, the studio's historical preference for white heroes and heroines remains a source of controversy. For some people, Disney Culture reads as white culture, and the Walt Disney Company is cast as a backer of traditional white America, its power, politics, and social values.

As the film scholar Jason Sperb highlights, one of the most difficult Disney works remains *Song of the South*. In 1939, the same year as the release of *Gone with the Wind*, Walt Disney purchased the rights to a romantic southern fiction by Joel Chandler Harris. A literary eulogy for the antebellum South, Harris's novel featured his popular character Uncle Remus. Walt appreciated *Song of the South* for how it captured a lost rural America, reminiscent of Marceline. Disney Studios set about turning Harris's book into a movie, mixing live action and cartoons. Despite reservations about its racial content, the studio released *Song of the South* starring James Baskett as the jolly Uncle Remus in 1946.

The movie began, "Out of the humble cabin, out of the singing heart of the Old South have come the tales of Uncle Remus, rich in simple truths, forever fresh and new," and it told the story of the black ex-slave Remus and his relationship with Charlie, a white boy. The romantic, nostalgic, and deeply conservative depiction of southern life offended liberal Americans, and the National Negro Congress picketed theaters. Outdated, clichéd stereotypes of African Americans abounded. The studio depicted plantation life as bucolic and savory, with slavery seeming more a pleasant friendship between two groups than a brutal power relationship. Despite an NAACP representative being consulted during the script-writing process, the end product seemed indulgent, uncritical, and unrealistic. The hugely popular "Zip-a-Dee-Do-Dah" song by Uncle Remus, with its scenes of dancing bees and hummingbirds, made light of slavery, the "satisfactual" more counterfactual, and very few African Americans at the time connected with the "wonderful feeling" of a "wonderful day." Recognizing such problems, the studio kept *Song of the South* firmly in the vault from the 1970s onward. Elsewhere, Disney has deleted Nubian centaurettes and pickaninny shiners from *Fantasia*. This process of careful editing highlights a corporation keen to maintain a good image and not offend minority groups. Similar to its Disneyfication of American history, any awkward parts of Disney's own past have been cleansed.

It is equally important to see Disney Culture as inextricably linked to dominant themes, actions, and prejudices of American culture of the day. Black Americans were barred from Disneyland as they were from other public venues in the 1950s. Disney remains very much part of the popular culture of its era, and other cartoon companies such as Hanna-Barbera produced equally offensive stereotypes. While sometimes reactionary, the studio has often promoted an ethos of harmony, happiness, and social progress conducive to better race relations. The company has also consciously addressed issues of racial balance in its film productions. Lead characters now include Pocahontas (Native American), Tiana (African American), Fa Mulan (Chinese), and Aladdin and Princess Jasmine (Middle Eastern), not forgetting Mowgli (Indian) from the original *Jungle Book* (1967).

DISNEY, SEXUALITY, AND GENDER

Disney also has a mixed record on the issue of gender. Arguably, the studio both empowers and restricts the female in its movies. *Mary Poppins* (1964) highlights how the corporation played to both chauvinist and feminist sympathies in the 1960s. While Robert Stevenson's film tackled suffragette issues (including a rousing "Votes for Women" song), it equally questioned that a woman dedicated to the feminist cause could be an effective mother. Mr. Banks, the business bore and head of the family, is instead challenged by the nanny (Julie Andrews), who herself mixes old-style family values and loyal servitude with personal empowerment.

This restrict-empower tactic is exemplified in the cultural phenomenon of the "Disney princess." The studio first introduced the princess as one of its signature characters in the movie *Snow White*, with a pretty domestic goddess (albeit one that employs nature to do all the work) being targeted by a vain Wicked Witch. In *Snow White*, women were depicted as facile, anxious, and helpless homemakers, while men played the role of servants, worshipers, and saviors of the "fairer" sex. *Snow White* nonetheless founded the "Disney princess" ideal. The "princess empire" continued with Cinderella and Aurora in the 1950s. Bound up in contemporary expectations of body type, sexuality, and male rescue, the promotion of the woman as "princess" proved highly problematic. Disney peddled fantasies of female life based around love on first sight, lasting marriage, and honorable princes. Such cartoon dreams remained ignorant of the realities of life, including issues such as loveless relationships.

In the 1990s, a range of new Disney princesses appeared on-screen. Female leads in *The Little Mermaid* (1989), *Pocahontas* (1995), and *Mulan* (1998) all demonstrated feminist qualities. Tiana from *Princess and the Frog* (2009) provided a strong lead role, while Merida from *Brave* (2012) rebutted many female stereotypes. The live-action/animated feature *Enchanted* (2007) parodied Disney's own princess myth through the escapades of Giselle. Supporters of Disney were suddenly able to present the company as the true home of female-based stories and to highlight how strong heroines and Burbank heritage went hand in hand. Compared to Pixar, which took seventeen years to introduce a female lead (not to mention traditional Hollywood male bias), Disney boasted a track record of putting women first, starting with its first movie. New Disney princesses no longer needed men to save or endorse them. They appeared part of third-wave feminism, supporting the reintroduction of romance, privilege, and femininity into the movement. Disney seemed the home of the empowered princess.

Peggy Orenstein pondered, "Maybe princesses are in fact a sign of progress, an indication that girls can embrace their predilection for pink without compromising strength or ambition; that, at long last, they can 'have it all.'" Princess costumes became costumes of power.

Disney stores also sold princess costumes in legion. The company coupled the new princess with consumption, recognized its princess range as a valuable commodity, and fervently sold "the princess dream." In 2000, the former Nike employee Andy Mooney introduced the "Disney Princess" franchise. The original lineup featured nine characters: Snow White, Cinderella, Aurora, Ariel, Belle, Jasmine, Pocahontas, Mulan, and Tinkerbell. By 2006, the company had licensed over twenty-five thousand Princess products. In real-life ceremonies at historic palaces, new princesses Tiana, Rapunzel, and Merida were inducted into the "hall of fame." Disney sold "girl power" as princess power. The modern female was lofted as a proud shopper and consumer, the wearing of a princess outfit no longer about playing bride but about bling, success, and status. Matching Disney prince outfits were conspicuous by their absence. Princesses were doing it for themselves.

The intense commercialization of the Disney princess revealed some of the problems and ambiguities of Disney role models. While films depicted more nuanced

characters, product lines of plastic dolls lacked sophistication, and many resembled simple stereotypes. Pack-
aged princess dolls for sale in Disney Stores appeared the
product of Hollywood makeovers with their lightened
skin tones (including a whiter Mulan and Pocahontas)
and perfect lithe bodies, and they hardly contested a
growing culture of plastic surgery and body dysmorphia.
Disney princesses made Barbie look feminist and realistic. Disney Stores encouraged a princess look and mentality for girls. The seemingly endless supply and demand
for Disney princesses left little room for anything else.
Disney Culture existed only as princess culture. This
monopoly over image left little choice of role models for
kids. As the artist Dina Goldstein in her "Fallen Princesses" photo essay maintains, people who are "wrapped
up in Disney princesses" need to have "their eyes open
a little wider to the world" (Odell). For Goldstein, the
studio spread a cultural blindness and naiveté about society. As the journalist Monika Bartyzel contended, Disney
offered a "narrow version of femininity." By 2015, with
Disney's purchase of Marvel and *Star Wars*, both franchises traditionally aimed at males, the Disney Princess
line remained the sole attraction targeting the female
audience. Disney Stores resembled segregated spaces of
childhood and sold reductive, problematic garments for
both boys and girls.

While feminists critiqued Disney for its backward imagery, American conservatives targeted the corporation for going too far in its progressive role. As a bastion of traditional family values, Walt Disney was cherished by conservative groups for his old-fashioned ways. In the 1990s, Disney's shift toward a more progressive line, as well as its purchase of more adult-oriented brands such as Miramax, alienated its core customers. A backlash grew. In 1995, the American Life League (ALL) alleged that Disney movies featured subliminal sexual messages. In 1996, the American Family Association (AFA) called for a boycott of the company on the basis of its ownership of Miramax and the controversial movie *Priest* (which depicted sexual relations among Catholic clergy). The ultraviolence of *Pulp Fiction*, another Miramax title, equally offended. The same year, the Southern Baptist Convention (SBC), with 15.7 million members and forty thousand churches, resolved to challenge Disney on its "anti-Christian and anti-family" content. With the studio's purchase of ABC and the comedy show *Ellen* in 1997, along with news of Gay Days at Disney World, the SBC led a conservative boycott of all Disney products as punishment for the corporation "increasingly promoting immoral ideologies" across America (Sutton 325). *Newsweek* reported SBC spokesperson Richard Land's "sense of betrayal and outrage" at Disney and his demand that the company pick sides: "You can't walk the family side of the street and the gay side of the street in the Magic Kingdom at the same time" ("Baptists vs. Mickey"). Land nicknamed WDW "the tragic kingdom," situating it as a ground zero in the battle between traditional conservative America and gay-friendly liberals (Reuters). WDW was labeled as "where the values of Hollywood and mid-America collide" (Myerson).

The shape of Disney Culture thus became part of a broader battle over American culture. Identified with liberal Hollywood, modern Disney seemed far from Walt's nostalgic Marceline. Meanwhile, Baptists were forced to make an active choice in their lives: Mickey Mouse or God. Turning off their televisions and canceling the Disney-owned sports channel ESPN, the more resolute members declared, "It will affirm to us and the world that we love Jesus more than we love our entertainments" (M. Miller). Others quietly left their cable on. Gay-rights groups defiantly labeled the boycott as "an attack on homosexuals that would fail" (Myerson). In June 2005, the AFA boycott ended on the pretense that the group had "made their point known" (Johnson). Wiley Gray from SBC Florida claimed, "We have cost them hundreds of millions of dollars" (Associated Press). Although Disney sold Miramax, little had really changed with regard to Disney's policies or its presentation of gender and sexuality. *Glee* (2010–15) proved highly popular with a gay audience. Arguably, the boycott had little effect, and "gay Disney" seemed stronger than ever. The end of the boycott appeared more suggestive of shifts in mainstream society. Disney Culture and mass American culture seemed more aligned again.

The release of *Frozen* in 2013 suggests that the studio may yet push further into liberal and progressive America and lead rather than lag in social values. Disney's adaptation of Hans Christian Andersen's "Snow Queen" transformed the story of two sisters into a story of female empowerment. Significantly, the two sisters rarely talked about boys or jewels. Like *Enchanted*, the movie mocked traditional myths, showing love at first sight as an illusion and men as very poor saviors. The studio challenged its own Cinderella stereotypes within the movie and, in the process, helped to reframe the Disney princess. Disney depicted the "family" as two sisters together, challenging its own past insistence on the traditional nuclear family led by mother and father. The movie boasted female leads and a female director (Jennifer Lee, teamed with Chris Buck), which complemented other movies of the period, such as *The Hunger Games*, and fed a new optimism about female Hollywood. *Forbes* magazine commented that, "gloriously animated, wonderfully acted, and refreshingly feminist," *Frozen* appeared "a turning point for the Mouse House" (Mendelson).

Frozen also appealed to a gay audience. Elsa is forced to conceal her difference before coming out defiantly, thus relating to a challenge faced by many Americans. "Let It Go" quickly became a coming-out song for a generation, with Elsa herself lauded as a gay hero. The movie scene "Wandering Oaken's Trading Post" was interpreted as suggestive of transgression and exploration, with owner Oaken taken by some viewers as the studio's first openly gay character. Such a gay-friendly reading of *Frozen* predictably offended conservative America. One Reformation Church pastor derided *Frozen* as "very evil," branding Disney "one of the most pro-homosexual organizations in the country," while the Catholic minister Steven Greydanus warned Catholics against the "gay culture themes" (Denham).

The movie also appealed as a commentary on adolescence and the challenges of growing up. "Let It Go" provided a liberation anthem for all and sundry, a rallying cry for anyone feeling rejected or oppressed. Rather than a depiction of conventional villains, emotions offered the real barrier in the movie to overcome. As the Broadway coauthor of "Let It Go" Kristen Anderson-Lopez explained, "Screw fear and shame, be yourself, be powerful"

(Ryzik). *Frozen* showed progressive, modern Disney at its best. The corporation seemed capable of leaving behind outdated values and jumping ship. Amassing $401 million in domestic receipts, *Frozen* proved Disney's highest grossing animation. Even Disney was shocked by the success. Critics had initially dismissed the movie, with Scott Foundas for *Variety* writing, "[*Frozen* is] longer on striking visuals than on truly engaging or memorable characters." Instead *Frozen* emerged as a cultural phenomenon. Families held *Frozen* parties and sing-alongs, and obsessive fans acted out role-play. *Frozen* seemed everywhere, especially in stores. Disney dominated family rooms and downtowns, and everyone loved it.

FUTURE DISNEY

In October 1968, the artist Ernest Trova, best known for his sculpture *The Falling Man*, gathered together materials for work on a "time capsule" of the twentieth century. Trova proclaimed the swastika, the Coca-Cola bottle, and Mickey Mouse as the three most important graphical images of the century and included in his time capsule a variety of examples of Mickey Mouse memorabilia (Bayer). The dominance of Mickey Mouse and Disney over the past one hundred years is staggering. As Fjellman notes, "to explain Walt Disney World, then, is to explain a good deal about twentieth-century America" (2).

Disney remains in the twenty-first century a pivotal force in American culture. However, the studio has changed a lot since Trova's time capsule. For one thing, the corporation is much larger, with a truly global business model and worldwide multimedia presence. It owns major franchises and television channels. Disney no longer carries an old-fashioned conservative reputation and potentially may alienate its white middle-class core. "Disney America" in the twenty-first century is fundamentally something quite different from Walt's America of the twentieth century.

Twenty-first-century Disney also has its problems. In response to the terrorist attacks of 9/11, the commentator Karen Moline predicted, "The ironic thing about 11 September is that people want comfort, and if anything Disney will become even more successful because what they represent is a Utopian vision of the US, as a place where you don't have to bother about locking your door or worry about having your office blown up by a terrorist" (BBC News). People needed Mickey Mouse post-9/11. However, while the company did grow post-9/11, the mouse itself proved curiously quiet in the first two decades of a new century. The studio instead brought in other characters from outside Walt's world, like Marvel superheroes and *Star Wars* jedi.

The silence of Mickey leaves a question mark over the studio's place in America. America is heavily invested in Disney. Not to believe in Disney is equivalent to not believing in the small-town America of old or a "happily ever after" in the future. Discarding Disney is tantamount to shredding the traditional American Dream and becoming decidedly un-American. The multimedia giant is just too important. But Disney needs to start being more than a financial giant and a holding company. Disney Culture needs to remain relevant. It needs purpose beyond corporate growth or story recycling. CEO Bob Iger consciously appointed John Lasseter and Ed Catmull from Pixar to head up Disney animation and to inject such direction after years of average movies. "I love and care so deeply about the people here," Lasseter reported, "and I love Walt Disney so much, and how he entertained me. I wanted to keep this studio going" (Roper). With *Frozen*, the studio seems capable of more. After decades of playing it safe, Disney Culture in the twenty-first century needs to challenge us. It needs to mean something beyond merchandise. Disney Culture is part of our heritage and our culture. Mickey needs to start saying something.

ACKNOWLEDGMENTS

My thanks to Chris Pallant at Christchurch University and Tom Lawrence at Kent University for reading and commenting on *Disney Culture*, as well as series editors Wheeler Winston Dixon and Gwendolyn Audrey Foster, and Leslie Mitchner and the staff at Rutgers University Press.

FURTHER READING

Allan, Robin. *Walt Disney and Europe: European Influences on the Animated Feature Films of Walt Disney*. Bloomington: Indiana University Press, 1999.

Apgar, Garry, ed. *A Mickey Mouse Reader*. Jackson: University Press of Mississippi, 2014.

Barrier, Michael. *Animated Man: A Life of Walt Disney*. Berkeley: University of California Press, 2008.

Bryman, Alan. *Disney and His Worlds*. London: Routledge, 1995.

Bryne, Eleanor, and Martin McQuillan. *Deconstructing Disney*. London: Pluto, 1999.

Finch, Christopher. *The Art of Walt Disney: From Mickey Mouse to the Magic Kingdoms*. New York: Abrams, 1973.

Fjellman, Stephen. *Vinyl Leaves: Walt Disney World and America*. Boulder, CO: Westview, 1992.

Foglesong, Richard E. *Married to the Mouse: Walt Disney World and Orlando*. New Haven, CT: Yale University Press, 2001.

Gabler, Neal. *Walt Disney: The Triumph of the American Imagination*. New York: Knopf, 2006.

Giroux, Henry. *The Mouse That Roared: Disney and the End of Innocence*. Lanham, MD: Rowman and Littlefield, 2010.

Jackson, Kathy Merlock, and Mark West, eds. *Disneyland and Culture: Essays on the Parks and Their Influence.* Jefferson, NC: McFarland, 2011.

———. *Walt Disney, from Reader to Storyteller: Essays on the Literary Inspirations.* Jefferson, NC: McFarland, 2015.

Knight, Cher Krause. *Power and Paradise in Walt Disney's World.* Gainesville: University Press of Florida, 2014.

Miller, Diane Disney. *The Story of Walt Disney.* New York: Holt, 1957.

Pallant, Chris. *Demystifying Disney: A History of Disney Feature Animation.* New York: Continuum, 2011.

Project on Disney. *Inside the Mouse: Work and Play at Disney World.* Durham, NC: Duke University Press, 1995.

Schickel, Richard. *The Disney Version: The Life, Times, Art and Commerce of Walt Disney.* 3rd ed. Chicago: Ivan R. Dee, 1997.

Smoodin, Eric, ed. *Disney Discourse: Producing the Magic Kingdom.* New York: Routledge, 1994.

Thomas, Bob. *Walt Disney: An American Original.* New York: Simon and Schuster, 1976.

Wasko, Janet. *Understanding Disney.* Cambridge, UK: Polity, 2001.

Watts, Steven. *The Magic Kingdom: Walt Disney and the American Way of Life.* New York: Houghton Mifflin, 1997.

WORKS CITED

Allan, Robin. *Walt Disney and Europe*. Bloomington: Indiana University Press, 1999.

Allen, David. "Disneyland: Another Kind of Reality." *European Journal of American Culture* 33.1 (2014): 33–47.

Allen, Stephanie. "Disney Dogged by Spiffy Transient, Deputies Allege." *Orlando Sentinel* 9 July 2015.

Andersen, Marthe A. "O.D.D. (Obsessive Disney Disorder)." Art video. Oslo, 2013. http://www.malcanisen .berta.me/art/o-d-d-obsessive-disney-disorder/.

Artz, Lee. "The Righteousness of Self-Centered Royals: The World According to Disney Animation." *Critical Arts* 18.1 (2004): 116–31.

Associated Press. "Southern Baptists End Disney Boycott." *Augusta Chronicle* 23 June 2005.

Banksy. "It's a Flawed Concept." Interview. 1 Sep. 2015 http://dismaland.co.uk/interview/.

"Baptists vs. Mickey." *Newsweek* 30 June 1997.

Barnes, Brook. "Disney Looking into Cradle for Customers." *New York Times* 6 Feb. 2011.

———. "Revamped Disney Park Tries Again." *New York Times* 15 June 2012.

Barrier, Michael. *The Animated Man: A Life of Walt Disney*. Berkeley: University of California Press, 2007.

Bartyzel, Monika. "Girls on Film: The Real Problem with the Disney Princess Brand." *The Week* 17 May 2013. http://theweek.com/articles/464290/girls-film-real-problem-disney-princess-brand.

Baudrillard, Jean. *America*. London: Verso, 1989.

———. *Simulations*. Semiotext(e), 1983.

Bayer, Ann. "Happy 40th, Mickey." *Life* 23 Oct. 1968.

BBC News. "Spotlight on Disney's Cultural Legacy." 5 Dec. 2001. http://news.bbc.co.uk/1/hi/entertainment/1693448.stm.

Bohas, Alexandre. "Disney: A Cultural Capitalism of Global Entertainment." *INAGlobal (Cinema)* 24 May 2011. http://www.inaglobal.fr/en/cinema/article/disney-cultural-capitalism-global-entertainment.

Breaux, Richard. "After 75 Years of Magic: Disney Answers Its Critics, Rewrites African American History, and Cashes In on Its Racist Past." *Journal of African American Studies* 14.4 (2010): 398–416.

"British Fear 'Snow White' Will Cause Nightmares." *New York Times* 6 Feb. 1938.

Brockway, Robert W. "The Masks of Mickey Mouse: Symbol of a Generation." *Journal of Popular Culture* 22.4 (Spring 1989): 25–34.

———. *Myth from the Ice Age to Mickey Mouse*. Albany: State University of New York Press, 1993.

Bryman, Alan. *The Disneyization of Society*. Thousand Oaks, CA: Sage, 2004.

Burks, Robin. "How Star Wars Has Taken Over Disneyland." *Tech Times* 25 Feb. 2016.

Burns, Ken. "TV Documentarian's Advice." *Potomac News* 24 May 1994.

Capodagli, Bill, and Lynn Jackson. *The Disney Way: Harnessing the Management Secrets of Disney in Your Company.* New York: McGraw-Hill, 2006.

Carr, Austin. "The Messy Business of Reinventing Happiness." *Fast Company* May 2015.

Cartnal, Alan. "Coming of Age at Disney All-Nite Show." *Los Angeles Times* 23 June 1971.

Cast-member. "IAmA former Disney Princess." reddit discussion group 28 Jan. 2012. https://www.reddit.com/r/IAmA/comments/pocdm/iama_former_disney_princess_ama/.

CBS. "The Sunny Side of the Atom." Radio broadcast. 30 Jun. 1947. Folder 14, Box 19, Papers of the Atomic Scientists of Chicago, Regenstein Library, University of Chicago.

Churchill, Douglas. "Disney's Philosophy." *New York Times* 6 Mar. 1938.

Coca-Cola. "Mission, Vision and Values." n.d. 10 Mar. 2016 http://www.coca-colacompany.com/our-company/mission-vision-values.

———. "Unique Culture." n.d. 10 Mar. 2016 http://www.coca-colacompany.com/careers/unique-culture.

Culhane, John. "A Mouse for All Seasons." *Saturday Review* 1 Nov. 1978.

Cypher, Jennifer, and Eric Higgs. "Colonizing the Imagination: Disney's Wilderness Lodge." *Capitalism Nature Socialism* 8.4 (1997): 107–30.

Debord, Guy. *The Society of the Spectacle*. 1967. Trans. Donald Nicholson-Smith. New York: Zone Books, 1994.

Denham, Jess. "Disney's Frozen Is 'Very Evil' Gay Propaganda, Says Christian Pastor." *Independent* 3 Mar. 2014.

Disney, Claire. Interview. *Hoarder Next Door*. Channel 4 Productions (TV), 2014.

Disney, Roy E., and Michael Eisner. "California Adventure Dedication." Televised footage. 8 Feb. 2001. https:// www.youtube.com/watch?v=75pwQhLK2yw.

Disney College Program. "The Disney Look." http:// cp.disneycareers.com/en/about-disney-college -program/disney-look/.

"Disney Hates Poor People." Thread on CoasterBuzz 18 June 2015. http://coasterbuzz.com/Forums/Topic/ disney-hates-poor-people.

Disney Institute. "Business Excellence." n.d. 10 Mar. 2016 https://disneyinstitute.com/courses/business -excellence/.

"Disney Invades 'Serious' Realm with Feature." *Los Angeles Times* 19 July 1938.

"Disney Joins the Masters in the Metropolitan." *New York Times* 24 Jan. 1939.

"Disneyland Gang Going to France." *Gadsden Times* 19 Dec. 1985.

"Disney's Four Keys to a Great Guest Experience." *Disney at Work* (blog) n.d. 10 Mar. 2016 http://disneyatwork .com/disneys-four-keys-to-a-great-guest-experience/.

Ducas, Dorothy. "The Father of Snow White." *Los Angeles Times* 19 June 1938.

Eco, Umberto. *Travels in Hyper-reality*. Basingstoke, UK: Picador, 1986.

Eisenstein, Sergei. *The Eisenstein Collection*. Ed. Richard Taylor. Calcutta: Seagull Books, 2006.

Eisner, Michael. *Work in Progress*. New York: Random House, 1998.

Eliot, Marc. *Walt Disney: Hollywood's Dark Prince*. Secaucus, NJ: Carol, 1993.

Feinberg, Scott. "Walt Disney's Grandniece Agrees with Meryl Streep: He Was 'Racist.'" *Hollywood Reporter* 15 Jan. 2014.

Fishwick, Marshall. "A Mouse of Influence around the World." *Orlando Sentinel* 14 June 1992.

Fjellman, Stephen. *Vinyl Leaves: Walt Disney World and America*. Boulder, CO: Westview, 1992.

Foglesong, Richard E. *Married to the Mouse: Walt Disney World and Orlando*. New Haven, CT: Yale University Press, 2001.

Forster, E. M. "Mickey and Minnie." *Spectator* 19 Jan. 1934.

Foundas, Scott. "Film Review: *Frozen*." *Variety* 3 Nov. 2013.

Giroux, Henry. *The Mouse That Roared: Disney and the End of Innocence*. Lanham, MD: Rowman and Littlefield, 2010.

Goffman, Erving. *Asylums: Essays on the Social Situation of Mental Patients and Other Inmates*. New York: Anchor Books, 1961.

Gould, Stephen Jay. "Mickey Mouse Meets Konrad Lorenz." *Natural History* 88.5 (May 1979): 30–36.

Grazer, Brian. "Inventing Worlds in a Changing One." Talk with J. J. Abrams and Jony Ive. *Vanity Fair* 9 Oct. 2015.

http://video.vanityfair.com/watch/the-new
-establishment-summit-jony-ive-j-j-abrams-and-brian
-grazer-on-inventing-worlds-in-a-changing-one-2015
-10-09.

Greenhouse, Steve. "Playing Disney in the Parisian Fields." *New York Times* 17 Feb. 1991.

Griffin, Sean. *Tinker Belles and Evil Queens*. New York: NYU Press, 2000.

Halevy, Julian. "Disneyland and Las Vegas." *Nation* 7 June 1958.

Harbord, Janet. *The Evolution of Film: Rethinking Film Studies*. Cambridge, UK: Polity, 2007.

Harwell, Drew. "How Theme Parks Like Disney World Left the Middle Class Behind." *Washington Post* 12 June 2015.

Hetter, Katia. "To Disney or Not to Disney?" CNN.com 5 Oct. 2015. http://edition.cnn.com/2013/03/22/travel/disney-travel-debate/.

"Historians vs. Disney." Thread on H-CivWar May 1994. http://www.chotank.com/disvasav2.html.

Holliss, Richard, and Brian Sibley. *The Disney Studio Story*. London: Octopus Books, 1988.

Hopper, Hedda. "Walt Disney Called All-Year Santa Claus." *Los Angeles Times* 25 Dec. 1956.

Horkheimer, Max, and Theodor W. Adorno. *Dialectic of Enlightenment*. Amsterdam: Querido Verlag, 1947.

Jameson, Fredric. "Postmodernism, or The Cultural Logic of Late Capitalism." *New Left Review* 1.146 (July–August 1984): 53–92.

Jamison, Barbara Berch. "Of Mouse and Man." *New York Times* 13 Sept. 1953.

Jenkins, Henry. *Convergence Culture: Where Old and New Media Collide*. New York: NYU Press, 2006.

Jensen, Jessica. "Wall-E: Robotic Ode to Environmental Protection." *Huffington Post* 25 May 2011. http://www.huffingtonpost.com/jessica-jensen/wall-e-robotic-ode-to-env_b_109847.html.

Johnson, M. Alex. "Southern Baptists End 8 Year Disney Boycott." NBCNews.com 22 June 2005. http://www.nbcnews.com/id/8318263/ns/us_news/t/southern-baptists-end--year-disney-boycott/#.VtmPuoR8-xo.

Johnston, Alva. "Mickey Mouse." *Woman's Home Companion* July 1934.

Jones, Bruce. "How Would You Respond If Asked: 'What Time Is the 3 O'Clock Parade?" *Disney Institute Blog* 9 June 2015. https://disneyinstitute.com/blog/2015/06/how-would-you-respond-if-asked-what-time-is-the-3-oclock-parade/355/.

"Keeping the Sheet Snow-White." *Manchester Guardian* 22 June 1939.

Kehr, Dave. "Its Not All Ooh-la-la over French Disney Park." *Chicago Tribune* 8 June 1991.

Keim, Brandon. "The Environmentalism of Wall-E." *Wired* 11 July 2008.

Knight, Cher Krause. *Power and Paradise in Walt Disney's World*. Gainesville: University Press of Florida, 2014.

Kotz, Nick, and Rudy Abramson. "The Battle to Stop Disney's America." *Cosmos* 1997. http://www.cosmosclub.org/journals/1997/disney.html.

Landry, Robert J. Review of *Steamboat Willie*. *Variety* 21 Nov. 1928.

Lewine, Edward. "Who Is He?" *New York Times* 10 Aug. 1997.

Lipton, Lawrence. *The Holy Barbarians*. New York: Julian Meaner, 1959.

Low, David. "Leonardo da Disney." *New Republic* 5 Jan. 1942.

Lukas, Scott A. "How the Theme Park Gets Its Power: Lived Theming, Social Control, and the Themed Worker Self." *The Themed Space: Locating Culture, Nation, and the Self.* Ed. Scott A. Lukas. Lanham, MD: Rowman and Little-field, 2007. 183–206.

Lush, Tamara. "'Celebration' Murder: Disney-Built Town Has Its First Killing Ever." *Huffington Post* 25 May 2011.

Lutts, Ralph. "The Trouble with Bambi: Walt Disney's *Bambi* and the American Vision of Nature." *Forest and Conservation History* 36 (Oct. 1992).

MacDonald, Brady. "Disney California Adventure: A Peek into What the Future May Hold." *Los Angeles Times* 13 Dec. 2010.

———. "Disney California Adventure: How We Got Here and What's Next." *Los Angeles Times* 18 June 2012.

Martens, Todd. "Happy Birthday to Disneyland, and to Tomorrowland's Forgotten Pig." *Los Angeles Times* 17 July 2015.

Martin, Hugo. "After Dark, the Dirty Work at Disneyland Begins." *Los Angeles Times* 2 May 2010.

Mendelson, Scott. "Review: 'Frozen' Is Disney's Triumphant Reaffirmation of Its Cultural Legacy." *Forbes* 19 Nov. 2013.

Mennel, Timothy. "Victor Gruen and the Construction of Cold War Utopias." *Journal of Planning History* 3.2 (May 2004): 116–50.

Miller, Diane Disney. "My Dad, Walt Disney, Part 2." *Saturday Evening Post* Nov. 1956.

Miller, Mike. "Action Isn't about 'Boycott,' It's about 'Moral Stewardship.'" *SBC Life* Sept. 1997. http://www.sbclife .net/Articles/1997/09/sla2.

Mills, C. Wright. *White Collar*. New York: Oxford University Press, 1951.

Mills, Eleanor. "I'm Not Doing Down Disney, Claims Banksy." *Sunday Times* 30 Aug. 2015.

Mooney, Andy. "The Disney Renaissance and the Culture Industry." *Disney: The Magic Empire* (blog) 13 Mar. 2012. http://disneythemagicempire.blogspot.co.uk/2012/ 03/disney-renaissance-and-culture-industry.html.

Mosley, Leonard. *Disney's World: A Biography*. New York: Stein and Day, 1985.

"Mouse and Man." *Time* 27 Dec. 1937.

Mouse Clubhouse. "Interview: Connie Swanson-Lane." YouTube 15 Oct. 2015. https://www.youtube.com/ watch?v=i3U2HDd7uE0.

Myerson, Allen R. "Southern Baptist Convention Calls for Boycott of Disney." *New York Times* 19 June 1997.

Nugent, Frank. "The Music Hall Presents Walt Disney's Delightful Fantasy." *New York Times* 14 Jan. 1938.

———. "One Touch of Disney." *New York Times* 23 Jan 1938.

Odell, Amy. "Why Are Adults on the Internet So Obsessed with Disney Princesses?" *Vanity Fair* 30 Aug. 2013.

Orenstein, Peggy. "What's Wrong with Cinderella?" *New York Times* 24 Dec. 2006.

Pallant, Chris. *Demystifying Disney: A History of Disney Feature Animation*. New York: Continuum, 2011.

Perez-Pena, Richard. "Disney Drops Plan for History Theme Park in Virginia." *New York Times* 29 Sept. 1994.

Pierce, Todd James. "In Defense of Walt: Walt Disney and Anti-Semitism." Disney History Institute 22 Feb. 2014. http://www.disneyhistoryinstitute.com/2014/02/in-defense-of-walt-walt-disney-and-anti.html.

Pilkington, Ed. "How the Disney Dream Died in Celebration." *Guardian* 13 Dec. 2010.

Powers, William. "Eisner Blasts Critics of Disney Virginia Park." *Washington Post* 14 June 1994.

"Premier Annoyed by Ban on a Visit to Disneyland." *New York Times* 20 Sept. 1959.

PR Newswire. "Disney's Animal Kingdom at Walt Disney World Resort Dedicated Tuesday in African-Themed Spectacle." 21 Apr. 1998. http://www.prnewswire.com/news-releases/disneys-animal-kingdom-at-walt-disney-world-resort-dedicated-tuesday-in-african-themed-spectacle-77522472.html.

Pryor, Thomas. "Land of Fantasia Is Rising on the Coast." *New York Times* 2 May 1954.

———. "Snow White Sidelights." *New York Times* 5 Feb. 1939.

Reuters. "Disney Boycott Escalated by Baptist Group." *Washington Post* 14 Aug. 1997.

Ritzer, George. *The McDonaldization Thesis: Explorations and Extensions.* Thousand Oaks, CA: Sage, 1998.

RKO-Pathe News. "Fantasy Filmland Thrills to 'Snow White.'" 1937.

Rodaway, Paul. "Exploring the Subject in Hyper-reality." *Mapping the Subject: Geographies of Cultural Transforma-*

tion. Ed. S. Pile and N. J. Thrift. New York: Routledge, 1995. 241–67.

Rojek, Chris. "Disney Culture." *Leisure Studies* 12.2 (1993): 121–35.

Roper, Caitlin. "*Big Hero 6* Proves It: Pixar's Gurus Have Brought the Magic Back to Disney Animation." *Wired* 21 Oct. 2014.

Russell, Herbert. "L'Affaire Mickey Mouse." *New York Times* 26 Dec. 1937.

Ryzik, Melena. "The Nominees Are Blockbusters." *New York Times* 19 Feb. 2014.

Schallert, Elza. "Radio Interview with Walt Disney." NBC 12 Mar. 1937. http://www.disneyhistoryinstitute.com/ 2011/12/happy-birthday-walt.html.

Scheuer, Philip. "Cartoon Films Develop Their Own Jargon." *Los Angeles Times* 8 Mar. 1936.

———. "Mickey Mouse Routs Comics from Screen." *Los Angeles Times* 21 June 1936.

Schumach, Murray. "Films by Disney Work Two Ways." *New York Times* 13 Nov. 1961.

Schwarz, Benjamin. "Walt's World." *Atlantic* Dec. 2006.

Scott, A. O. "In a World Left Silent, One Heart Beeps." *New York Times* 27 June 2008.

Shaffer, Rosalind. "A Visit to Walt Disney's Plant." *Chicago Tribune* 23 Feb. 1936.

"Snow White Continues to Be Popular Fare." *Los Angeles Times* 14 Mar. 1938.

"Snow White Hailed as Big Step Forward." *Los Angeles Times* 9 July 1938.

Southern Baptist Convention. "Resolution on Disney Company Policy." New Orleans, LA. 1996. http://www.sbc.net/resolutions/435.

Sperb, Jason. *Disney's Most Notorious Film: Race, Convergence, and the Hidden Histories of "Song of the South."* Austin: University of Texas Press, 2012.

Stroud, Dick. "World's Fair Report: Walt Disney." Radio interview. 1964. https://www.youtube.com/watch?v=PuonSVNCpZE.

Sutton, Jerry. *A Matter of Conviction: A History of Southern Baptist Engagement with the Culture.* Nashville, TN: Broadman, 2008.

Thomas, Bob. *Walt Disney: An American Original.* New York: Simon and Schuster, 1976.

Tinee, Mae. "'Snow White' Fulfills Very Hope of Every Critic." *Chicago Tribune* 5 Mar. 1938.

Tomkins, R. "Fair Game for a Gentle Savaging." *Financial Times* 25 Apr. 1998.

Updike, John. Introduction. *The Art of Mickey Mouse.* Ed. Craig Yoe and Janet Morra-Yoe. Los Angeles: Hyperion, 1991. N.p.

Walt Disney Company. "Animal Kingdom." Guest brochure. Mar. 2013.

———. "Plans Unveiled for 'Disney's America' Near Washington DC." News release. 11 Nov. 1993. http://chotank.com/reledisn.html.

———. "Welcome to Golden Oak." Commercial. 2013. https://www.youtube.com/watch?v=Q3inHlZabro.

Walt Disney Studios. "Our Friend the Atom." Season 3, episode 14. *Disneyland.* Television broadcast. 23 Jan. 1957.

————. *What Is Disneyland.* Television program. 27 Oct. 1954.

Warner, Gary. "Original D.C.A. Review: 'Sequel Is No Equal.'" *Orange County Register* 26 Mar. 2015.

Wasko, Janet. *Understanding Disney.* Cambridge, UK: Polity, 2001.

WED Enterprises. Disneyland prospectus/brochure. Burbank, CA: WED, 1953.

Whitley, David. *The Idea of Nature in Disney Animation.* Aldershot, UK: Ashgate, 2008.

Willett, Megan. "A Former 'Snow White' Dishes about Life as a Disney Park Princess." *Business Insider* 23 Oct. 2015. http://www.businessinsider.co.id/a-former-disney -princess-tells-all-2013-4/11/#.VthIMIR89Eg.

Will.i.am. Interview. *Harrods Man* 3 (Apr. 2015).

Williams, Whitney. "Mary Poppins." *Variety* 28 Aug. 1964.

Wills, John. *US Environmental History: Inviting Doomsday.* Edinburgh: Edinburgh University Press, 2012.

Wilson, Alexander. *The Culture of Nature: North American Landscape from Disney to the Exxon Valdez.* Toronto: Between the Lines, 1991.

INDEX

ABOUT THE AUTHOR

John Wills is a senior lecturer in American history and currently the director of American studies at the University of Kent, United Kingdom, where he teaches courses in US cultural and environmental history. His books include *Invention of the Park: From the Garden of Eden to Disney's Magic Kingdom* (2005), *Conservation Fallout: Nuclear Protest at Diablo Canyon* (2006), *The American West: Competing Visions* (2009), and *US Environmental History: Inviting Doomsday* (2012). He is the winner of the 2003 C. L. Sonnichsen Award for best article in the *Journal of Arizona History* and, since 2009, the editor of the *European Journal of American Culture.*